# THE DICTIONARY OF
# ESSENTIAL
# AMERICAN SLANG

by Peter Tse

Optima Books

Berkeley, California

Optima Books
2820 Eighth Street
Berkeley, CA 94710

ISBN 1-879440-29-6

First printing 2000
Printed in the United States of America

# Introduction

The purpose of this dictionary is to provide students of American English a list of the essential slang words and phrases used in everyday conversations.

I spent many years teaching English as a foreign language, first in the Peace Corps in Nepal, and then for five years in Japan. My students asked to be taught the English that native speakers actually use, rather than the stuffy English taught in textbooks. This concise guide to slang (no dead or obscure words) was written with these students in mind, and the terms and expression listed here will be understood by almost every adult native speaker in the United States.

There is not always a clear line separating slang from standard English. While the distinction is obvious for most vulgar or obscene words, other terms originally considered to be slang are in everyday use and exist in a hazy zone between accepted words and slang. Because this dictionary is intended for the intermediate-level student, I have included many of these words as long as I felt that the reader would benefit.

The student can use this book as a regular dictionary or as a study guide since only commonly used words are included.

Each boldface entry includes a definition in standard English and a pronunciation using the International Phonetic Alphabet. Example sentences (often the very sentence that I heard in a conversation) are used to illustrate typical usage of the term. Slang words used in the example sentences and found elsewhere in the dictionary are underlined so that the reader can look up their meanings. Expressions related to the main term are listed in small capitals at the bottom of each entry.

The grammatical type of most words or phrases is given as follows:

>*adj* = adjective or adjective phrase
>
>*adv* = adverb or adverbial phrase
>
>*conj* = conjunction
>
>*contr* = contraction
>
>*exp* = idiomatic expression
>
>*imp* = imperative
>
>*int* = intensive
>
>*inter* = interjection
>
>*n* = noun or noun phrase
>
>*prep* = preposition
>
>*v* = verb or verb phrase

Some slang words in this dictionary are innocuous, while others are vulgar and offensive. A numbering system has been used to rank the various expressions. (Note that these ratings are subjective. Other speakers may differ on ranking.)

❶ non-offensive slang that can be used in casual situations

❷ the cute slang of children

❸ the slang of teenagers and young adults

❹ mildly vulgar or crude slang

❺ very vulgar, offensive slang

❻ hateful and extremely insulting

Always employ common sense in using these words, particularly those rated ❹ through ❻. In the wrong situation, you could deeply offend someone or even get hurt. On the other hand, every native speaker knows these words, and you will hear them at the movies and on the street at times.

I hope your study of English will benefit from my years of jotting down the living slang words and expressions of the United States. Your spoken English will become more natural, and your comprehension of real American English will improve as you learn the words that make English teachers shudder.

Have fun and *get psyched!*

Peter Tse

# Pronunciation Guide

## Simple Vowels

| | sound | IPA |
|---|---|---|
| i | hit | hit |
| iː | mean | miːn |
| e | said | sed |
| æ | sat | sæt |
| æː | bag | bæːg |
| ər | clear | kliər |
| əːr | bird | bəːrd |
| ə | sofa | sóufə |
| ʌ | fun | fʌn |
| ɑ | fox | fɑks |
| ɑː | palm | pɑːm |
| ɔ | cough | kɔf |
| ɔː | call | kɔːl |
| u | book | buk |
| uː | boot | buːt |

## Dipthongs

| | sound | IPA |
|---|---|---|
| iər | deer | diər |
| ei | say | sei |
| ɛər | bear | bɛər |
| ai | fly | flai |
| au | now | nau |
| ɔi | boy | bɔi |
| ou | blow | blou |
| uər | sure | ʃuər |

## Consonants

| | sound | IPA |
|---|---|---|
| p | pill | pil |
| b | bill | bil |
| t | till | til |
| d | dill | dil |
| k | kill | kil |
| g | gill | gil |
| m | mill | mil |
| n | nil | nil |
| ŋ | drink | driŋk |
| l | little | lídl |
| f | fill | fil |
| v | verb | vəːrb |
| θ | thing | θiŋ |
| ð | that | ðæt |
| s | sill | sil |
| z | zoo | zuː |
| ʃ | shoot | ʃuːt |
| ʒ | genre | ʒáːnrə |
| h | hill | hil |
| j | young | jʌŋ |
| w | will | wil |
| r | red | red |
| tʃ | chill | tʃil |
| dʒ | Jill | dʒil |

# A

**AC/DC** [eísiːdíːsi] *adj* bisexual ❸

I don't think he's completely gay. He's probably **AC/DC**.

**ace** [eis] *adj* masterful, superior ❶

My son's a <u>total</u> superstar. The <u>guy's</u> an **ace** basketball player, swimmer, and scholar.

**ace** [eis] *v* to perform perfectly ❶

I **aced** that test.

**act** [ækt] *n* a pretense, an effected performance ❶

I don't think he's <u>really</u> sick. I'm sure it's an **act**. He just wants some sympathy.

> see also: SCHTICK, SPIEL

**acting up** [æktiŋ ʌp] *v* to malfunction, behave badly ❶

The engine's been **acting up** lately, so I came in to have it checked out.

Johnny kept **acting up** in class <u>and stuff</u> so Mr. Smith <u>like</u> called his mother.

My illness **acts up** whenever I'm under stress.

**action** [ækʃən] *n* excitement ❸

<u>Man</u>, this party's, <u>like</u>, <u>really</u> boring. Let's <u>cruise</u> to where the **action** is.

1

We're <u>gonna</u> go look for some **action**.

Where's the **action** around here?

**ad** [æd] *n* advertisement    ❶

Look at this **ad** in the paper.

**"adios"** [ɑdːjóus] *inter* [from Spanish] used to express    ❶
farewell

**Adios** <u>amigos</u>. I'm <u>gonna</u> <u>head out</u> now.

  see also:  CIAO, I'M OUT OF HERE, LATER, SEE YA, TAKE IT EASY

**adorable** [ədɔ́ːrəbəl] *adj* cute, charming    ❶

<u>God</u>, this puppy's so **adorable**!

**after** [ǽftər] *prep* in pursuit of    ❶

He's not so much **after** fame as he is after power.

What's he **after**?

The <u>cops</u> are **after** me.

**ages** [éidʒəz] *n* a long time    ❶

<u>Wow</u>, I haven't seen you in **ages**! How've <u>ya</u> been?

**ain't** [eint] *contr* [from *are not, am not, is not*] (Note    ❸
that use of this word tends to make the speaker sound
uneducated)

I **ain't** <u>gonna</u> go tomorrow.

He says he **ain't** hungry.

Ya **ain't** <u>gonna</u> tell on me are <u>ya</u>?

He **ain't** been here yet.

You **ain't** seen 'em, have <u>ya</u>?

**ain't worth shit** [eint wərθ ʃit] *adj* worthless   ❹

A: Joe said he'd buy me a diamond ring if I go out with him.

B: Anything he tells you **ain't worth shit**, girl. The guy's a total bullshit artist.

**airhead** [ɛ́ərhed] *n* mindless or stupid person   ❸

What do you wanna go out with an **airhead** for?

That girl's a total **airhead**. I'll bet she can't even count to five.

see also:  BIRDBRAIN, BLOCKHEAD, BONEHEAD, BOZO, CRETIN, DIMWIT, DINGBAT, DITZ, DODO, DOPE, DUMBELL, DUMMY, GOOF, GOOFBALL, KNUCKLEHEAD, LAMEBRAIN, MEATHEAD, NINCOMPOOP, NUMBSKULL, PEA-BRAIN, RETARD, SCATTERBRAIN, SPACE CADET, TWIT

**all over (the place)** [ɔːl óuvər] *adv*, *n* everywhere,   ❶
throughout

I looked **all over** for you! Where were you?

There was blood **all over the place**.

His presentation was **all over the place**. He should have organized it better.

see also:  EVERY WHICH WAY, HERE AND THERE

**already** [ɔːlrédi, ɔːrédi] *int* expression of urgency or   ❶
irritation

Cut it out **already**, will ya!

Get outta here **already**!

Stop it **already**, will ya!

Enough **already**!

**amigo(s)** [əmíːgou] *n* friend [from Spanish]   ❶

Yo **amigo**, you know the name of this town?

**ammo** [ǽmou] *n* [from *ammunition*]  ❶

We're running out of **ammo**, and the enemy is approaching. What should we do?

The other Party won the election '<u>cuz</u> they used the scandal as **ammo**.

**an'** [æn, en, ən] *conj* [from *and*]  ❶

I saw '<u>em</u> **an'** said "hi".

**an arm and a leg** [ənármənəlég] *exp* a large  ❶
amount, a lot

This car cost me **an arm and a leg**.

I paid **an arm and a leg** for this leather jacket, but I think it's worth it.

    see also: BUNCH, SHITLOAD, TON

**animal** [ǽniməl] *n* a person exhibiting characteristics  ❸
typically applied to animals

He's an **animal**! All he ever wants to do is sleep, eat, and have sex.

    see also: DOG, PIG

**antsy** [ǽntsiː] *adj* nervous  ❶

He always gets **antsy** before skydiving.

    see also: HIGH-STRUNG, UPTIGHT

**anyway** [éniwei] *adv* nevertheless, at any rate  ❶

Tickets weren't cheap, but, **anyway**, the concert was <u>like</u>, the best.

I don't care if it's raining. I <u>wanna</u> go **anyway**.

**Anyway**, what were we talking about before the phone rang?

**ask for it** [ǽsk fər it] *v* to put oneself at risk ❶

His wife ditched him, but he was **asking for it**. He cheated on her a million times.

The president of the company was <u>really</u> **asking for i**t when he started having an affair with his secretary.

**ass** [æs] *n* buttocks, behind ❹

That dude's got a fat **ass**.

<u>Check it out</u>! She's got a <u>hot</u> **ass**.

see also:  BOTTOM, BUM, BUNS, BUTT, FANNY, HEINIE, REAR END

**ass** [æs] *n* selfish, foolish person ❹

Why did you have to act like such an **ass**?

<u>Man</u>, sometimes you're a total **ass**.

see also:  JERK

**ass backwards** [æs bǽkwərdz] *adj* wrong, ❹
completely opposite

You got it **ass backwards** <u>baby</u>. I don't hate you, I love you.

**asshole** [ǽshoul] *n* the anal sphincter ❺

I'm <u>gonna</u> shove this computer up your **asshole** if you don't quit bugging me.

**asshole** [ǽshoul] *n* a despicable person ❺

<u>Fuck you</u>, **asshole**!

Hey **asshole**, come here and say that to my face!

<u>God</u>, I hate working for that **asshole**!

see also:  BASTARD, COCKSUCKER, CREEP, DICK, DICKWEED, DIP, DIPSHIT, DOUCHE BAG, FUCK, FUCKER, JERK, MOTHERFUCKER, PRICK, SCHMUCK, SOB, SON OF A BITCH

**ass kisser** [ǽskisər] *n* a sycophant ❹

I hate the way he always brings the teacher presents.
He's such an **ass kisser**.

see also: BROWNNOSER

**attaboy/attagirl** [ǽdəbɔi, ǽdəgərl] *exp* [from *that's* ❶
*my boy*, *that's my girl*] used to praise or encourage

**Attaboy** Johnnie, you're doin' just fine.

**attitude** [ǽdituːd] *n* a conceited or arrogant manner ❸

<u>Man</u>, that <u>girl's</u> got **attitude**. She don't take <u>shit</u> from
nobody!

see also: COCKY, HIGHFALUTIN', SNOOTY, SNOTTY, STUCK UP,
UPPITY

**attitude problem** [ǽdituːd práblem] *n* a poor or ❶
inappropriate attitude

<u>Ya</u> know, you got a <u>real</u> **attitude problem** my friend.
What makes you think you're so special?

**awesome** [ɔ́ːsəm] *adj* great, impressive ❸

<u>Wow</u>, this stereo's <u>totally</u> **awesome**. It must put out a
thousand watts!

She's got this new, <u>like</u> <u>really</u> **awesome**, boyfriend.

see also: BAD, BADASS, CRAZY-ASS, EXCELLENT, INTENSE, OUT
OF SIGHT, OUT OF THIS WORLD, RAD, SUPER, TO DIE
FOR, WILD

**"awesome!"** [ɔ́ːsəm] *inter* "Fantastic!" "Impressive!" ❸

**Awesome!** <u>Check out</u> Peter's new car!

see also: AWESOME, DYNAMITE, EXCELLENT, FAR OUT, GREAT,
OUT OF SIGHT, RIGHT ON, WOW

# B

**babe** [beib] *n* a sexy or attractive person, also used as ❸
a term of address

Man, check out that **babe** over there in the blue jeans.

He's such a **babe**! No wonder the ladies love him.

   see also:  BROAD, CHICK, GIRL, STUD

**baby** [béibi] *n* someone who complains or cries easily ❶

You're such a **baby**. Every time you get hurt, even a
little, you cry.

**baby** [béibi] *n* intimate companion ❸

My **baby** left me and now I'm feeling pretty down.

**baby** [béibi] *n* a term of address ❸

Hey **baby**, want to go get some Chinese? I'm starving.

   see also:  HONEY, LOVEY, SWEETIE

**back** [bæk] *v* to operate a car in reverse ❶

Tell the driver to **back** the truck up to the loading
dock.

**back** [bæk] *v* to support ❶

He won the election because he was **backed** by
powerful people.

**back down** [bæk dáun] *v* to give in, surrender ❶

At first it looked like the two gangs were gonna have a
fight, but then one of them **backed down** and
everything was cool.

**back off** [bæk ɔːf] *v* to retreat ❶

Initially, Tom insisted on the adoption of his proposal at the meeting, but he **backed off** when he realized people were getting <u>pissed off</u> at him.

**"back off!"** [bæk ɔːf] *imp* "Retreat!" "Get away!" ❶

The bodyguard yelled **"back off!"** when someone tried to touch the President.

**back out (on)** [bæk áud ɑn] *v* to break a ❶
commitment

You can't **back out on** us now. We're counting on you.

He's trying to **back out** of the agreement we signed last year.

see also:  BAG IT, BLOW OFF, CHICKEN OUT, COLD FEET, COP OUT, DITCH, WALK OUT ON, WIMP OUT

**back (someone) up** [bæk ʌp] *v* to provide support ❶

<u>Man</u>, I'm counting on you to **back me up** if there's a fight.

**backstabber** [bǽkstæbər] *n* a false friend who betrays ❶
a trust

You **backstabber**! Why did you tell my boyfriend I went to another <u>guy's</u> house?

see also:  FINK, RAT

**bad** [bæd] *adj* good, great ❸

<u>Man</u>, your new car is **bad**!

see also:  AWESOME, BADASS, CRAZY-ASS, EXCELLENT,  INTENSE, OUT OF SIGHT, OUT OF THIS WORLD, RAD, SUPER, TO DIE FOR, WILD

**bad** [bæd] *adj* tough, threatening ❸

  A: That <u>asshole</u> was <u>hittin' on</u> my girlfriend. I'm <u>gonna</u> <u>kick his ass</u>.

  B: I'm tellin' you <u>man</u>, don't <u>mess around with</u> him. He's one **bad** <u>motherfucker</u>.

    see also:  BADASS, MEAN

**badass** [bǽd æs] *adj* tough, impresssive ❹

  They've got this <u>real</u> **badass** car that can go 120 MPH.

    see also:  BAD, COOL, MEAN, SLICK

**baddie (the)** [ðə bǽdiː] *n* one who enforces the rules, ❶ the "heavy"

  Why do I always have to be the one to punish the kids? I'm tired of having to be **the baddie** all the time!

**bad egg** [bæd eg] *n* a rotten person ❷

  He's the only **bad egg** in the family. The rest are good people.

**bad-mouth** [bǽdmauθ] *v* to criticize severely ❶

  I dislike people who act nice to your face, but then **bad-mouth** you behind your back.

  He's always **bad-mouthing** his company. Why doesn't he just quit <u>already</u>?

**bad news** [bæd nuːz] *n* unwelcome situation or ❶ person

  Only two weeks in New Orleans and we've been <u>mugged</u> twice. This place is **bad news**.

  That <u>dude</u> is **bad news**. Invite him to the party and there'll be a <u>big scene</u> <u>for sure</u>.

## bad scene/big scene [bæd siːn] *n* an unpleasant ❶
experience, exhibition of anger

If my father comes home and finds you in the house, there's <u>gonna</u> be a <u>real</u> **bad scene**. And I <u>ain't</u> joking. He'll kill you.

> see also:  SCENE, STINK, TO-DO

## bad trip [bæd trip] *n* a bad experience, sometimes ❸
drug-related

A: What happened? You look like hell.

B: We all got high on some <u>bad</u> <u>shit</u>. Lou was havin' a real **bad trip**, so we took him to the hospital. He nearly <u>OD'd</u>.

## bag it [bǽg it] *v* to quit, to abandon ❶

We decided to **bag it** after we realized how much money it would cost to buy a house.

> see also:  BACK OUT, BLOW OFF, CHICKEN OUT, COLD FEET, COP
> OUT, DITCH, WALK OUT ON, WIMP OUT

## ball buster [bɔ́ːl bʌstər] *n* someone or something that ❹
gives one trouble or makes one work hard

My boss is a <u>real</u> **ball buster**.

Writing this book was a <u>real</u> **ball buster**.

> see also:  BITCH

## balls [bɔːlz] *n* testicles ❹

That <u>guy's</u> pants are so tight you can see his **balls**.

She kicked him in the **balls** and ran away.

## balls [bɔːlz] *n* courage ❹

<u>Ya</u> <u>gotta</u> have **balls** to <u>wanna</u> climb the Himalayas.

> see also:  CHUTZPAH, GUTS

**ballsy** [bɔ́ːlziː] *adj* courageous ❹

James Bond is <u>really</u> **ballsy**. Nothing scares him.

see also: GUTSY

**baloney** [bəlóuniː] *n* nonsense ❶

<u>Dad</u>, I don't believe in Santa Claus. It's just some **baloney** grown-ups made up.

see also: BULLSHIT, CRAP, GARBAGE, JIVE, RUBBISH, TRASH

**bam** [bæm] *n* a dull resounding noise

I heard the **bam** when your car hit the pothole! ❶

see also: BANG, BOOM, KABOOM, WHAM

**bam!** [bæm] *adv* with violent abruptness ❶

The rock hit her on the head and **bam!** she was dead.

see also: BANG, BOOM, KABOOM, POW, WHAM

**bang** [bæŋ] *v* to knock or hit ❶

He **banged** the crook on the head with a baseball bat and killed him.

Two <u>guys</u> **banged** into me and one of them tried to pick my pocket.

She was angry and **banged** the door as she left.

see also: BASH, BOP, WHACK

**bang** [bæŋ] *v* to have sex with ❺

She's <u>totally</u> sexy. I would love to **bang** her.

see also: FUCK, HUMP, LAY, MAKE LOVE, PORK, SCREW

**barf** [baːrf] *v, n* to throw up or vomit ❸

Oh <u>gross</u>! Somebody **barfed** all over the bathroom!

11

Careful, there's **barf** all over the floor!

see also:  BOOT, HEAVE, PUKE, THROW UP

**barge into** [baːrdʒ intuː] *v* to enter abruptly or ❶
rudely

The cops **barged into** the gangsters' headquarters and arrested everybody.

I just hate the way she always **barges into** other people's conversations.

**bash** [bæʃ] *v* to hit ❶

She **bashed** the robber on the head with a frying pan.

see also:  BANG, BOP, WHACK

**bash** [bæʃ] *n* a party, celebration ❶

There was a <u>real</u> **bash** over at Tom's last night, with dancing and <u>tons</u> of beer.

see also:  TO-DO

**basket case** [bǽskitkeis] *n* a crazy person, one who is ❶
completely incapacitated

She's become a <u>real</u> **basket case** since she started doing drugs.

The economic situation in my company? <u>Forget it</u>. The place is a **basket case**.

see also:  FREAK, FRUITCAKE, KOOK, NUTCASE, ODDBALL,
SCREWBALL, WEIRDO, WHACKO

**bastard** [bǽstərd] *n* a despicable person ❺

Your father was a no-good **bastard**. He drank, gambled, and <u>womanized</u>.

That **bastard** forgot to tip me!

see also:  ASSHOLE, COCKSUCKER, CREEP, DICK, DICKWEED, DIP,
DIPSHIT, DOUCHE BAG, FUCK, FUCKER, JERK,
MOTHERFUCKER, PRICK, SCHMUCK, SOB, SON OF A BITCH

**battle-ax** [bǽdl æks] *n* a crabby, old woman  ❸

There was no room on the train, but the old **battle-ax** shoved her way on <u>anyway</u>.

see also:  BITCH, OLD BAG

**batty** [bǽdiː] *adj* crazy, eccentric  ❶

Ignore what she says. She's just a **batty** old lady.

see also:  BONKERS, KOOKY, LOONEY, NUTS, OFF THE WALL, OUT IN LEFT FIELD, OUT THERE, OUT TO LUNCH, SCREWY, WAY-OUT, WHACKED-OUT, WHACKO, WHACKY

**bawl one's eyes out** [bɔːl wʌnz áz aut] *v* to cry  ❶
loudly and continuously

She **bawled her eyes out** when she got her test back with an "F" on it.

**bawl (someone) out** [bɔːl aut] *v* to criticize loudly  ❶

The boss <u>really</u> **bawled me out** when I showed up late to work again.

see also:  CHEW SOMEONE OUT, COME DOWN ON SOMEONE, JUMP ALL OVER, JUMP ON, LET SOMEONE HAVE IT, RAG ON, TAKE IT OUT ON

**beak** [biːk] *n* nose  ❶

<u>Check out</u> the huge **beak** on that guy over there.

see also:  SCHNOZZ

**beat** [biːt] *adj* tired  ❶

After studying English for three hours I was pretty **beat**.

see also:  BLEARY-EYED, BURNED OUT, BUSHED, DEAD, FRAZZLED, FRIED, OUT OF IT, POOPED, WASTED, WIPED OUT, ZONKED OUT

**"beat it!"** [bíːd it] *imp* "Get out of here!"  ❹

Hey you! What <u>the hell</u> are you doin' sittin' on my car! **Beat it!**

13

**beat-up** [biːt ʌp] *adj* old and dilapidated ❶
   A: You still driving that piece of <u>shit</u>?
   B: Hey, my car's pretty **beat-up**, but it still runs.
   A: If I were you I'd junk it.

   see also: CHEWED UP, RUN-DOWN

**beaut (a)** [ə bjúːt] *n* [from *beautiful*] a beautiful ❶
example

   <u>Wow</u>, that horse is a <u>real</u> **beaut**! I'll bet he could win
   the Kentucky Derby!

**beautiful** [bjúːdiful] *adj* perfect, exciting ❶

   <u>Wow</u> <u>man</u>, that homerun was beautiful!

   see also: AWESOME

**beaver** [bíːvər] *n* the vagina ❺

   I'm <u>gonna</u> go get myself some **beaver** tonight.

   see also: CUNT, PUSSY

**"because I say so"** [bikɔ́z ai séi sou] *exp* "Because I ❶
have the authority!"

   A: Clean up your room!
   B: Why?
   A: **Because I say so**. Now do it!

**beer belly** [bíər béliː] *n* a paunch from drinking too ❶
much beer

   I'll never get rid of this **beer belly** if I don't stop
   drinkin' so much beer.

   see also: GUT

**belly button** [bélibʌtən] *n* navel ❷

   She'll <u>freak out</u> if you touch her **belly button**.

**belly-up** [béli: ʌp] *adj* out of business, bankrupt ❶

The company went **belly-up** last year.

see also: BROKE, KAPUT

**bent out of shape** [bent aut əv ʃéip] *exp* angry, ❶
upset

Why are you getting so **bent out of shape**? It was just a joke.

see also: PISSED OFF, TICKED OFF

**big deal** [big díːl] *n* an important event (sometimes ❶
used sarcastically)

Why are you so upset about getting a parking ticket?
It's not such a **big deal**.

Whenever she looks at another man her boyfriend gets
insanely jealous. He makes a **big deal** out of it and they
have a big fight.

**"big deal"** [big díːl] *inter* "So what?" or "I'm not ❶
impressed"

A: Yesterday I picked up a French model at a bar and
she's crazy about me.

B: **Big deal**.

**big mouth** [big máuθ] *n* person who talks too much, ❸
one who gossips

I can't believe what a **big mouth** you have! How could
you tell him I like him!

You can't tell him anything '<u>cuz</u> he's a **big mouth**.

see also: TRAP

**big shot** [big ʃɑt] *n* an important or influential person ❶

You've sure got an <u>attitude</u>. You act like you think
you're a **big shot** or something.

see also: HEAD HONCHO, HEAVY, VIP

**big spender** [big spéndər] *n* someone who spends a  ❶
lot, often to impress others

A: I hate the way that <u>dude</u> tries to come across like
he's some kind of **big spender**. He's never bought
me nothin'!

B: That's <u>'cuz</u> you <u>ain't</u> a girl.

**big stink** [big stiŋk] *n* public outcry  ❶

The workers made a **big stink** when they found out
wages would be cut.

There was a **big stink** when the government tried to
censor the press.

**big-time** [bígtaim] *adj*, *adv* serious, seriously,  ❶
top-level

He's a **big-time** basketball star.

I think he's in **big-time** trouble.

We <u>screwed up</u> **big-time**.

He insulted her **big-time**.

> see also:  MAJOR, REAL

**bike** [baik] *n* motorcycle  ❶

The motorcycle gang raced their **bikes** across town <u>'cuz</u>
the <u>cops</u> were chasin' <u>'em</u>.

**bimbo** [bímbou] *n* a sexually attractive but  ❸
empty-headed woman

At first I liked her <u>'cuz</u> I thought she was pretty, but
when I realized she was just a silly **bimbo** I forgot about
her.

> see also:  EASY RIDE, HUSSY, NYMPHO, SLUT

**bind** [baind] *n* a difficult situation, in trouble   ❶

You've <u>gotta</u> help me. I'm in a real **bind** '<u>cuz</u> I've got no money and I've <u>gotta</u> pay my monthly loan payment tomorrow or the bank will repossess my car.

She was in a **bind** because she knew she would have to testify against her friend.

> see also:  HOT WATER, IN DEEP SHIT, JAM, TIGHT SPOT, UP SHIT'S CREEK

**"bingo!"** [bíŋgou] *inter* "Success!" or "Correct!"   ❶

**Bingo!** You win the jackpot!

A: You mean my boyfriend lied to me?
B: **Bingo!** He lies to everybody.

**birdbrain** [bə́rd brein] *n* a stupid person   ❸

Hey **birdbrain**, how come you don't get it?

He can't add. He's a <u>real</u> **birdbrain**.

> see also:  AIRHEAD, BLOCKHEAD, BONEHEAD, BOZO, CRETIN, DIMWIT, DINGBAT, DITZ, DODO, DOPE, DUMBELL, DUMMY, GOOF, GOOFBALL, KNUCKLEHEAD, LAMEBRAIN, MEATHEAD, NINCOMPOOP, NUMBSKULL, PEA-BRAIN, RETARD, SCATTERBRAIN, SPACE CADET, TWIT

**bitch** [bitʃ] *n* a nasty woman, a difficult situation or task   ❹

I hate the way that **bitch** is always telling me what to do.

<u>Man</u>, that test was a <u>real</u> **bitch**. I bet I didn't pass.

> see also:  BATTLE AXE, OLD BAG

**bitch** [bitʃ] *v* to complain   ❹

Why are you always **bitching** about Larry? You should be thankful you have such a good man for a husband.

> see also:  CARRY ON, GO ON AND ON, GRIPE, SOUND OFF

**blab** [blæb] *v* to talk aimlessly or excessively   ❶

He's constantly **blabbing** on the <u>phone</u>.

see also:   GAB, YAK, YAP

**blah blah blah** [bla bla bláː] *exp* [describes a   ❶
long-winded or foolish conversation]

She just kept talking, **blah blah blah**, about her
problems.

**blahs (the)** [ða bláːz] *n* a depressed or dark mood   ❶

Whenever it's cold and dark out, she gets the **blahs**.

see also:   BLUES, BUMMED OUT, DOWN, FUNK

**blast** [blæst] *n* enjoyable, exciting experience   ❶

I had a real **blast** driving those bumper cars.

A: Your party last night was a **blast**.
B: I'm surprised you remember it. You were pretty
<u>damn</u> <u>wasted</u>.

see also:   GAS, PISSER, RIOT

**bleary-eyed** [bliəriː aid] *adj* having the eyes dim and   ❶
watery from fatigue

I studied all night and was **bleary-eyed** during the
exam.

see also:   BEAT, BURNED OUT, BUSHED, DEAD, FRAZZLED, FRIED,
OUT OF IT, POOPED, WASTED, WIPED OUT, ZONKED OUT

**blimp/blimpo** [blimp, blímpou] *n* insulting term   ❸
for a fat or overweight person

He's become a <u>total</u> **blimpo** since he stopped
exercising.

see also:   FATSO, PORKER

**blind** [blaind] *adj* ignorant, unaware ❶

Some guys are **blind** to the dangers of VD. They think AIDS is something the "other guy" gets.

Don't be **blind**, girl. Can't you see he's just using you so he can get his hands on your roommate?

**blind date** [blaind deit] *n* a date between persons ❶ who have not previously met

We met on a **blind date**, believe it or not.

**blissed out** [blist aut] *adj* very happy ❸

Everybody at the concert was **blissed out** on sunshine and love.

**blockhead** [blákhed] *n* stupid person ❸

Hey **blockhead**, your socks are different colors.

see also: AIRHEAD, BIRDBRAIN, BONEHEAD, BOZO, CRETIN, DIMWIT, DINGBAT, DITZ, DODO, DOPE, DUMBELL, DUMMY, GOOF, GOOFBALL, KNUCKLEHEAD, LAMEBRAIN, MEATHEAD, NINCOMPOOP, NUMBSKULL, PEA-BRAIN, RETARD, SCATTERBRAIN, SPACE CADET, TWIT

**blow a hairy** [blouwəhéəriː] *v* to get very angry, to ❸ throw a tantrum

My <u>dad</u> **blew a hairy** when he found out I borrowed his car without asking.

see also: BLOW ONE'S COOL, FLIP, FREAK, GO APESHIT, GO BANANAS, GO POSTAL, LOSE IT, LOSE ONE'S COOL

**blow away** [blou əwéi] *v* to shock or amaze, beat ❶ badly, kill

I was **blown away** by that movie. It <u>really</u> moved me.

The Yankees **blew** <u>'em</u> **away** with a score of 31 to 3.

The cops **blew away** the bank robber.

see also: BLOW ONE'S MIND, FLOORED

**blow it** [blóu it] *v* to waste a good opportunity ❶

I could have gone to college, but I **blew it**. Instead I joined the army.

The Red Sox had a two run lead but they **blew it** and the other team won.

see also: LOSE OUT ON, MISS THE BOAT

**blow job** [blóujɑb] *n* fellatio ❺

We consulted the *Kama Sutra* on how to give a good **blow job**.

She gave Bill the best **blow job** he'd ever had.

see also: GIVE ONE HEAD, GO DOWN ON

**blow off** [blou ɔːf] *v* to disregard a commitment or ❶
responsibility

I was supposed to go to the meeting but I **blew** it **off** and saw a movie instead.

I can't believe you didn't show up for our date yesterday! You just **blew** me **off**!

see also: BACK OUT, CHICKEN OUT, COLD FEET, COP OUT, DITCH, WALK OUT ON, WIMP OUT

**blow off steam** [blou ɔːf stíːm] *v* to release tension ❶

I'm sorry I lost my temper earlier. I was just **blowing off steam** when I yelled at you. I've been under a lot of stress lately.

**blow one's cool** [blou wʌnz kúːl] *v* to get angry, to ❸
lose one's composure

A: <u>Holy shit</u>, there's a <u>cop</u> car comin', and we're in the middle of a <u>deal</u>.

B: Hey <u>man</u>, don't **blow your cool** and the <u>cops</u> will never find out.

A: <u>Oh my God</u>! Throw that <u>shit</u> away and let's run!

20

B: <u>Shut the fuck up</u>, and just look like you're walkin' down the street.

see also: BLOW A HAIRY, FLIP, FREAK, GO APESHIT, GO BANANAS, GO POSTAL, LOSE IT, LOSE ONE'S COOL

## blow one's cover [blou wʌnz kʌ́vər] *v* to reveal ❶
one's true identity

My girlfriend **blew my cover** when she called me by my real name.

## blow one's mind [blou wʌnz máind] *v* to amaze, ❸
to overwhelm

It **blew my mind** when I realized I had won the lottery.

I think he says shocking things just to **blow people's minds**.

see also: BLOW AWAY

## blues (the) [ðə bluːz] *n* a state of depression, low ❸
spirits

A: She's got **the blues** <u>'cuz</u> her boyfriend dumped her.

B: Yeah, well the only way to get over **the blues** is to get another <u>guy</u>.

see also: BLAHS, BUMMED OUT, DOWN, FUNK

## bod [bɑd] *n* [from *body*] body, figure ❸
She's got a really nice **bod**.

## bogus [bóugis] *adj* fake, untrue, insincere ❸
He gave me this <u>totally</u> **bogus** excuse for why he didn't come home last night.

see also: FAKE, PHONY

## boiling [bóiliŋ] *adj* very hot ❶
This room is **boiling**! Can I turn on the air conditioner?

## bond [bɑːnd] v to make a connection  ❶

I don't want to get an old dog. I want to get a puppy so it will **bond** with me.

The men go away every year for a week of fishing without their wives for some male-**bonding**.

see also: CLICK, CONNECT

## bonehead [bóunhed] n a dumb person  ❸

Don't put water in the gas tank, you **bonehead**!

see also: AIRHEAD, BIRDBRAIN, BLOCKHEAD, BOZO, CRETIN, DIMWIT, DINGBAT, DITZ, DODO, DOPE, DUMBELL, DUMMY, GOOF, GOOFBALL, KNUCKLEHEAD, LAMEBRAIN, MEATHEAD, NINCOMPOOP, NUMBSKULL, PEA-BRAIN, RETARD, SCATTERBRAIN, SPACE CADET, TWIT

## boner [bóunər] n an erection  ❹

He can't get a **boner** when he's under a lot of stress.

see also: HARD-ON, WOODY

## bonkers [bánkərz] adj crazy  ❶

My <u>old man</u> went **bonkers** when he found out I'd <u>totaled</u> his car.

I wouldn't listen to anything that guy says. He's **bonkers**.

see also: BATTY, KOOKY, LOONEY, NUTS, OFF THE WALL, OUT IN LEFT FIELD, OUT THERE, OUT TO LUNCH, SCREWY, WAY-OUT, WHACKED-OUT, WHACKO, WHACKY

## boo-boo [búː buː] n a slight injury  ❷

Mommy, mommy, do you have a bandage? I have a **boo-boo** on my knee.

## boobs [buːbz] n breasts  ❹

She's got the biggest **boobs** in town.

see also: KNOCKERS, TITS

**boob tube** [búːb tuːb] *n* television, TV ❶

I would rather read a novel than watch the garbage that's usually on the **boob tube**.

**booger** [búgər] *n* hardened mucus ❸

Oh gross! There's a **booger** coming out of his nose!

see also: SNOT

**boogie** [búgiː] *v* to move fast, leave quickly ❶

We'd better **boogie** if we want to make it on time.

see also: BOOK, CLEAR OUT, HAUL ASS, HIGHTAIL IT, HUSTLE, SPLIT, STEP ON IT, VAMOOSE

**book** [buk] *v* to arrest ❶

The cops **booked** him for pushing drugs.

see also: BUST

**book** [buk] *v* to move fast ❶

We're going to have to **book** if we want to make it to the airport on time.

see also: BOOGIE, CLEAR OUT, HAUL ASS, HIGHTAIL IT, HUSTLE, SPLIT, STEP ON IT, VAMOOSE

**boom!** [buːm] *adv* with violent abruptness ❶

The explosion went **boom!** Suddenly, there were bodies lying all over the place.

see also: BAM, BANG, KABOOM, WHAM

**boom box** [búːmbɑks] *n* a loud, portable stereo ❶

I was listening to my **boom box** on the subway but the transit cop told me to turn it off.

see also: GHETTO BLASTER

**boondocks/boonies** [búːndɑks, búːniz] *n* a rural ❶
area, a remote area far from a city

That guy comes from the **boondocks** somewhere out in
Idaho.

    see also:  STICKS

**boot** [buːt] *v* to throw up, vomit ❸

He **booted** <u>all over</u> the inside of the train.

    see also:  BARF, HEAVE, PUKE, THROW UP

**boot** [buːt] *v* to eject or discharge ❶

Why don't you **boot** your roomate if he's such a
nuisance?

    see also:  KICK OUT

**booze** [buːz] *n* liquor ❶

There wasn't any **booze** at the party, so we went out
and bought some.

**bop** [bɑp] *v* to hit ❶

She **bopped** him on the head with a frying pan.

    see also:  BANG, BASH, WHACK

**boss** [bɔs, bɑs] *v* to give arbitrary orders ❶

Who do you think you are, **bossing** everybody around?
You're just a new employee.

**bossy** [bási, bɔ́siː] *adj* domineering ❶

Nobody likes her <u>cuz</u> she's so **bossy**. She acts like she
owns the place.

**bottom** [bádəm] *n* buttocks ❶

When the pervert pinched the girl on the **bottom**, she turned around and <u>whacked</u> him across the face.

see also: ASS, BUM, BUNS, BUTT, FANNY, HEINIE, REAR END

**"bottoms up!"** [bàdəmz ʌ́p] *inter* "Cheers!" a ❶
drinking toast

**Bottoms up!** There's plenty more beer where that came from!

**bozo** [bóuzou] *n* a fool ❸

Who's that **bozo** going through my trash? Hey you! Get <u>the fuck</u> out of here!

see also: AIRHEAD, BIRDBRAIN, BLOCKHEAD, BONEHEAD, CRETIN, DIMWIT, DINGBAT, DITZ, DODO, DOPE, DUMBELL, DUMMY, GOOF, GOOFBALL, KNUCKLEHEAD, LAMEBRAIN, MEATHEAD, NINCOMPOOP, NUMBSKULL, PEA-BRAIN, RETARD, SCATTERBRAIN, SPACE CADET, TWIT

**brain** [brein] *n* a highly intelligent person ❸

Danny's a <u>real</u> **brain**. He <u>aces</u> every test.

**brains** [breinz] *n* intelligence ❶

That kid's got **brains**. She can play several chess games at the same time.

**brat** [bræt] *n* a spoiled child ❶

That kid's a **brat**. His mother should smack him when he acts like that, don't you think?

see also: SNOT

**brawl** [brɔːl] *n* a quarrel or noisy fight ❶

There was a **brawl** at the party, and the <u>cops</u> had to break it up.

**bread** [bred] *n* money ❸

> A: Hey <u>man</u>, you're lookin' pretty <u>down and out</u>.
>
> B: I <u>ain't</u> got enough **bread** to even buy me a goddamned cup of coffee. Got any spare change?
>
> A: Sorry <u>man</u>, I'm <u>broke</u> myself.
>
> see also: DOUGH, MOOLA

**break** [breik] *n* a chance, a respite, a temporary delay ❶

> Please just give me a **break**, <u>OK</u>? and I'll pay you back as soon as I can.
>
> I got the job?! This could be the big **break** I've been waiting for.
>
> see also: SLACK

**breakdown** [bréik daun] *n* a psychological collapse ❶

> He had a nervous **breakdown** after his wife left him.

**"break it up!"** [breik it ʌ́p] *imp* "Stop fighting!" ❶

> <u>OK</u> fellas, **break it up**, or I'll arrest both of <u>ya</u>!

**break one's balls** [breik wʌnz bɔ́ːlz] *v* to struggle or work very hard, to tease ❹

> A: Why's Larry got those circles under his eyes all the time?
>
> B: He's been **breaking his balls** working two jobs so he can feed his kids.
>
> see also: BUST ONE'S BALLS, BUST ONE'S BUTT, CRANK, HUSTLE, KNOCK ONESELF OUT

**break out** [breik áut] *v* to have an outbreak of acne ❶

> My face keeps **breaking out**. I look like a pizza.

**break up** [breik ʌp] *v* to end a relationship  ❶

They had been going out for two years and then suddenly **broke up**.

see also: SPLIT UP

**breeze** [briːz] *n* something easily accomplished  ❶

You'll have no trouble passing the driver's exam. It's a **breeze**.

see also: CINCH, PIECE OF CAKE, SNAP

**broad** [brɔːd] *n* derogatory term for woman or girl  ❹

Some stupid **broad** hit me with her car.

see also: BABE, CHICK, GIRL

**broke** [brouk] *adj* penniless, without money  ❶

The company's **broke**. You'd better quit now before it goes <u>belly-up</u>.

I'm **broke**. I can't afford to buy a car.

see also: FLAT BROKE, PISS-POOR

**brownnose** [bráun nouz] *v* to curry favor  ❸

Look at the way that <u>creep</u> talks to the professor after class. He's just **brownnosing** so he can get an A.

see also: KISS ASS, SUCK UP TO

**brownnoser** [bráun nouzər] *n* one who curries favor ❸

The boss is surrounded by **brownnosers** and yes-men.

see also: ASS KISSER

**brutal** [brúːdəl] *adj* extreme, difficult , cruel  ❶

This weather is **brutal**. It's so hot I can't stand it.

He said something <u>real</u> **brutal** to her and now she's crying.

**buck** [bʌk] *n* one US dollar ❶

You owe me thirty **bucks**. Please pay me back as soon as you can, <u>OK</u>?

**bud** [bʌd] *n* [from *buddy*] man, friend, also term of ❶ address

Eric and Scott are **buds**.

Hey **bud**, where's the nearest liquor store?

    see also:   DUDE, GUY, MAN

**buddy-buddy** [bʌ́diːbʌ́diː] *adj* friendly ❶

They've been **buddy-buddy** ever since high school.

    see also:   CHUMMY

**bug** [bʌg] *v* to annoy ❶

Stop **bugging** your sister. Can't you see that she's trying to do her homework?

    see also:   HASSLE, PESTER

**"bug off!"** [bʌg ɔ́ːf] *imp* "Go away!" ❸

**Bug off!** I'm trying to finish this book!

    see also:   DROP DEAD, GET LOST

**built** [bilt] *adj* having a well-proportioned body ❸

<u>Wow</u>, that <u>guy</u> is really **built**. He looks like a body builder.

    see also:   CUT, IN SHAPE

**bullshit** [búlʃit] *n* nonsense ❹

His resume is full of **bullshit**. He's never worked at any of these places!

    see also:   BALONEY, CRAP, FULL OF IT, GARBAGE, JIVE, RUBBISH, TRASH

**bullshit** [búlʃit] *v* to talk nonsense with the intention ❹
of deception

He **bullshitted** his way into the company by giving
false information on his resume.

I want you to stop **bullshitting** me and tell me the
truth.

    see also:  CON, SWEET TALK

**"bullshit!"** [búlʃit] *inter* "Nonsense!" said to challenge ❹
a statement

**Bullshit!** I think you're lying!

    see also:  BALONEY, GARBAGE

**bullshit artist** [búlʃit àrdist] *n* one who habitually ❹
exaggerates and talks nonsense

In order to be a successful politician you've <u>gotta</u> be a
**bullshit artist**.

**bum** [bʌm] *n* buttocks, behind ❸

She's got a real cute **bum**.

    see also:  ASS, BOTTOM, BUNS, BUTT, FANNY, HEINIE, REAR END

**bum** [bʌm] *n* a beggar, a person who lives in the street ❶

Some **bum** asked her for money, so she gave him some
change.

**bum** [bʌm] *v* to obtain by begging ❸

He **bummed** a cigarette off me.

**bum** [bʌm] *adv* to be depressed ❸

We were **bumming** after losing our third straight game.

29

**bum around** [bʌm əráund] *v* to spend time ❸
wandering

We **bummed around** Paris for a few weeks just having
fun.

see also: HANG AROUND

**bum deal** [bʌm diːl] *n* bad situation ❸

When the company went <u>belly-up</u>, all of us got a **bum
deal**. We never got our last paycheck!

see also: RAW DEAL

**bummed** [bʌmd] *adj* depressed ❸

We were both **bummed** after the concert was cancelled.

Hey <u>man</u>, you look really **bummed**. Is something the
matter?

see also: BLAHS, BUMMED OUT, DOWN, FUNK, OUT OF IT

**bummed out** [bʌmd áut] *adj* depressed ❸

He was **bummed out** for weeks after his college
application was rejected.

see also: BLAHS, BLUES, BUMMED, DOWN, FUNK

**bummer** [bʌ́mər] *n* a depressing situation ❸

I can't believe you didn't get into college. That's a <u>real</u>
**bummer** <u>man</u>.

see also: DOWNER, DRAG, PITS

**bump into** [bʌmp íntuː] *v* to encounter, to meet by ❶
accident

I **bumped into** my old high school girlfriend last night
at a party. We hadn't seen each other in ten years.

**bump (someone) off** [bʌmp sʌmwʌn ɔf] v to kill ❶

The mafia **bumped him off** because he was an informer.

see also: WASTE

**bunch** [bʌntʃ] n a considerable amount, a group ❶

I have a **bunch** of <u>stuff</u> to do before I go home.

A **bunch** of us went to see a movie.

see also: SHITLOAD, TON

**buns** [bʌnz] n buttocks ❸

A: I'd like to bite the **buns** on that <u>guy</u>.

B: <u>Yeah</u>? well, he's my boyfriend, so <u>back off!</u>

see also: ASS, BOTTOM, BUM, BUTT, FANNY, HEINIE, REAR END

**burbs** [bərbz] n [from *suburbs*] suburban neigborhood ❶

City life is too dangerous. I prefer living in the **burbs**.

**burned** [bə:rnd] *adj* hurt ❸

You say you love me? Well, I don't believe you. I think you're <u>full of it</u>. I've been **burned** too many times.

**burned out** [bə:rnd áut] *adj* exhausted or tired from ❸
working hard

A: I need a vacation. I'm feeling <u>real</u> **burned out**.

B: <u>Yeah</u>, me too. Nothin' but work, work, work and bills, bills, bills.

see also: BEAT, BLEARY-EYED, BUSHED, DEAD, FRAZZLED, FRIED,
OUT OF IT, POOPED, WASTED, WIPED OUT, ZONKED OUT

**burp** [bə:rp] n a release of gas from the stomach ❶

Did you eat Kimchee again? Your **burp** smells like garlic.

**burp** [bəːrp] *v* to make a noise when releasing gas ❶
from the stomach

Do you have to **burp** so loudly? That's <u>really</u> rude!

**bushed** [buʃt] *adj* tired, exhausted ❶

I'm <u>really</u> **bushed**. I just worked two shifts straight.

see also: BEAT, BLEARY-EYED, BURNED OUT, DEAD, FRAZZLED,
FRIED, OUT OF IT, POOPED, WASTED, WIPED OUT,
ZONKED OUT

**bust** [bʌst] *v* to arrest ❶

The cops **busted** everybody in the gang.

see also: BOOK

**bust one's balls** [bʌst wʌnz bɔːlz] *v* to work very ❹
hard

I'm a doctor now because I **busted my balls** in college.

see also: BREAK ONE'S BALLS, BUST ONE'S BUTT, CRANK, HUSTLE,
KNOCK ONESELF OUT

**bust one's butt** [bʌst wʌnz bʌt] *v* to work very ❹
hard

I **bust my butt** trying to make you happy, and all you
do is complain.

see also: BREAK ONE'S BALLS, BUST ONE'S BALLS, HUSTLE, KNOCK
ONESELF OUT

**butch** [butʃ] *adj* masculine in manner or appearance ❸

That woman is pretty **butch**. I wonder if she's a
lesbian.

see also: DYKE

**butt** [bʌt] *n* buttocks ❸

That guy's got a cute **butt**.

Get your **butt** over here right now!

see also: ASS, BOTTOM, BUM, BUNS, FANNY, HEINIE, REAR END

**buy** [bai] *v* to believe, to accept ❶

You're saying he's a movie actor? I just don't **buy** it.

**buzz** [bʌz] *n* the initial feeling of intoxication caused ❶
by alcohol or drugs

This pot gives you a strong **buzz**, but then it wears off
in half an hour.

see also: CHARGE, RUSH

# C

**call** [kɔ:l] *n* decision or ruling ❶

Hey, it's your **call**, <u>man</u>. I have no way of knowing
which way to decide.

**call (something) off** [kɔ:l sʌmθiŋ ɔ:f] *v* to cancel ❶

We had to **call the picnic off** because it was raining.

**can** [kæn] *v* to eliminate, to cancel ❶

The network **canned** the show after just one season.

see also: BAG IT, DITCH

**can** [kæn] *n* the toilet ❸

I <u>gotta</u> go to the **can**.

see also: JOHN

**carbos** [kárbouz] *n* [from carbohydrates] easily ❶
digested sugars and starches.

I'm running a marathon the day after tomorrow, so I
have to eat a lot of **carbos** today, you know, like
spaghetti <u>and stuff</u>.

**carry on (and on)** [kæriː ɔ́n ən ɔn] *v* to complain ❶
endlessly

Margaret was **carrying on and on** about how her
boyfriend <u>sleeps around</u> on her. I think she should just
leave the <u>bum</u>.

   see also:  CARRY ON, GO ON AND ON, GRIPE, SOUND OFF

**catch** [kætʃ] *n* concealed difficulty, penalty ❶

Listen to this <u>ad</u>: "Six CDs for only one penny." The
**catch** is that you have to buy ten more at the regular
price.

   see also:  DOWNSIDE, SMALL PRINT

**catch** [kætʃ] *n* a good find ❶

Tommy was a good **catch**. She's lucky he married her.

**catch on** [kætʃ ɔ́n] *v* to become popular ❶

E-mail really **caught on** in the 1990's. Now everybody
uses it.

**catch on** [kætʃ ɔ́n] *v* to understand ❶

I didn't realize that the doctor was lying to me. But
when I **caught on**, boy was I mad!

   see also:  FIGURE OUT, GET IT

**catch some z's** [kætʃ sʌm zíːz] *v* to sleep ❸

I'm <u>beat</u>. I think I'll go **catch some z's**.

   see also:  CONK OUT, SNOOZE

**champ** [tʃæmp] *n* [from *champion*] the winner in ❶
a competition; term of address

Mohammed Ali was the **Champ** after the "Thrilla in Manilla."

Hey **champ**, ready for today's assignment?

**charge** [tʃɑrdʒ] *n* an exciting feeling ❸

I love espresso in the morning. It gives me a <u>real</u> **charge**.

My neighbor gets a <u>real</u> **charge** out of beating his dog, so I called the police about it.

see also: BLAST, BUZZ, RUSH

**cheap** [tʃiːp] *adj* stingy ❶

He's <u>really</u> **cheap**. He gave his wife an imitation diamond for their twenty-fifth anniversary.

**cheapskate** [tʃíːpskeit] *n* a stingy person ❶

He's a <u>real</u> **cheapskate**. He asked me to pay for dinner, and he's the one who invited me!

see also: TIGHTWAD

**cheat** [tʃiːt] *v* to be unfaithful ❶

His wife said she wanted a divorce when she found out he was **cheating** on her.

see also: FOOL AROUND ON, SLEEP AROUND, TWO-TIME

**"check it out!"** [tʃek it áut] *inter* "Look at that!" ❶

<u>Wow</u>! **Check it out!** Her new boyfriend has a Ferrari. It's <u>awesome</u>!

see also: GET A LOAD OF

**check out** [tʃek aut] *v* to inspect ❶

He's always **checking out** the blondes at the beach.

35

I'm interested in buying your car, but I want to **check** it **out** before I buy it.

> see also:  EYEBALL, SCOPE

**cheesy** [tʃíːziː] *adj* of an old or ugly style, in bad taste  ❷

A: My parents listen to **cheesy** music from twenty years ago.

B: Yeah, I can't stand that <u>hippie</u> stuff.

> see also:  CORNY

**chewed up** [tʃuːd ʌp] *adj* damaged  ❶

I'm not going to buy this carpet. It's all **chewed up**.

> see also:  BEAT-UP, RUN-DOWN

**chew someone out** [tʃuː sʌmwʌn áut] *v* to  ❶
criticize harshly

A: When the boss caught her taking stamps from the office, he <u>really</u> **chewed her out**.

B: Well, he had every right to do that, <u>cuz</u> she was stealing from him.

> see also:  BAWL SOMEONE OUT, COME DOWN ON SOMEONE,
> JUMP ALL OVER, JUMP ON, LET SOMEONE HAVE IT, RAG
> ON, TAKE IT OUT ON

**chick** [tʃik] *n* insulting term for a woman or girl  ❹

Whoa! <u>Check out</u> that **chick** with the long legs over there.

> see also:  BABE,  BROAD, GIRL

**chicken** [tʃíkən] *n* a coward  ❶

I can't believe a **chicken** like Tom had the <u>guts</u> to climb this cliff.

> see also:  FRAIDY-CAT, GUTLESS WONDER

**chicken** [tʃíkən] *adj* cowardly ❶

He's terrified of the dark. He's so **chicken** he sleeps with a light on.

see also: GUTLESS

**chicken out** [tʃíkən aut] *v* to lose one's nerve ❶

They were engaged for a year and were supposed to get married, but on the wedding day he **chickened out** and didn't show up at the church.

see also: BACK OUT, BAG IT, BLOW OFF, COLD FEET, COP OUT, DITCH, WALK OUT ON, WIMP OUT

**chill** [tʃíl] *v* to relax ❸

A: What if he doesn't show up with our pay?

B: Let's just **chill** for a while till he shows up.

We were **chillin'** over at my friend's house.

see also: HANG, HANG OUT, TAKE IT EASY

**"chill out!"** [tʃíl áut] *imp* "Relax!" "Calm down!" ❹

A: **Chill out** <u>man</u>! Don't yell in my restaurant.

B: This <u>guy</u> was <u>hitting on</u> my wife.

A: Hey, if you're going to <u>make a scene</u>, go outside, otherwise keep your voices down, <u>OK</u>?

see also: COOL IT, COOL OUT

**chink** [tʃiŋk] *n* a very insulting term for someone of ❻ Asian ancestry

"Go back to China, you **chink**" is what that horrible man said to me.

**chintzy** [tʃíntsi:] *adj* cheap and inexpensive looking ❶

I can't believe you paid a hundred bucks for this dress. It's so **chintzy**.

see also: CRAPPY

**chip in** [tʃɪp ín] *v* to contribute ❶

<u>OK</u>, the bill is three hundred <u>bucks</u>. Since there are ten of us, each has to **chip in** thirty dollars.

We can paint this house in one day if everybody **chips in**.

**choke** [tʃouk] *v* to perform poorly under pressure ❸

I <u>really</u> **choked** on that exam.

**choked up** [tʃoukt ʌ́p] *adj* emotional and near tears ❶

He was all **choked up** and nearly cried as he watched his daughter get married.

**chow** [tʃau] *n* food ❸

<u>Ya</u> got any **chow**? I'm starving!

Let's go get some **chow**.

see also: GRUB, MUNCHIES

**chow down** [tʃau daun] *v* to eat ravenously ❸

I'm starving. Let's go someplace and **chow down**.

see also: PIG OUT, PORK OUT

**"Christ!"** [kraist] *inter* expression of anger, frustration, ❹ surprise

**Christ!** I can't believe you're late to your own wedding Everybody's waiting!

see also: DAMN, FOR CHRISTSAKE, GOD, JESUS CHRIST

**chummy** [tʃʌ́miː] *adj* friendly, on good terms ❶

He tries to stay **chummy** with people in positions of power.

see also: BUDDY-BUDDY

**chump** [tʃʌmp] *n* a fool ❶

You must think I'm a **chump**! I'm not going to lend you any more money because you never pay me back.

see also: SUCKER

**chutzpah** [hútspɑ] *n* nerve, supreme self-confidence ❶

He started his own company when he was just twenty-three. That takes <u>real</u> **chutzpah**.

see also: BALLS, GUTS

**"ciao"** [tʃau] *inter* [from Italian] "Goodbye" ❶

**Ciao**. I'll see you guys later.

see also: ADIOS, I'M OUTTA HERE, LATER, SEE YA, TAKE IT EASY

**cinch** [sintʃ] *n* something easily accomplished ❶

It'll be a **cinch** to get an A in this course.

see also: BREEZE, PIECE OF CAKE, SNAP

**class** [klæs] *n* style, elegance ❶

I like a girl with **class**.

He has no **class**.

see also: STYLE

**class act** [klæs ækt] *n* a person with style and elegance ❶

That guy is a <u>real</u> **class act**. He always brings roses to his wife on payday.

**classy** [klǽsiː] *adj* stylish, elegant ❶

This is a real **classy** restaurant, so don't slurp your soup.

**clean** [kliːn] *adj* no longer using drugs or alcohol ❶

I used to be addicted to heroin, but now I'm **clean**.

see also: STRAIGHT

**clean up** [kliːn ʌp] *v* to make a lot of money ❶

A: I **cleaned up** when I bought that stock. It doubled in value overnight!

B: Really! In that case, you can pay for dinner tonight.

**clear out** [kliər áut] *v* to leave quickly ❶

When the police came, all the crooks **cleared out**.

see also: BOOGIE, BOOK, HAUL ASS, HIGHTAIL IT, HUSTLE, SPLIT, STEP ON IT, VAMOOSE

**click** [klik] *v* to fit together, function smoothly ❶

We really **clicked** with each other. I guess we have the same sense of humor.

see also: BOND, CONNECT

**clincher** [klíntʃər] *n* a decisive fact or argument ❶

I suspected that my husband was cheating on me. The **clincher** was when I found another woman's lipstick on his pajamas.

**clingy** [klíŋiː] *adj* overly dependent and needy ❶

I can't stand how **clingy** he is around his mother. He's a real mama's boy.

**clit** [klit] *n* [from *clitoris*] ❺

She loves it when you pet her **clit**.

**clobber** [klábər] *v* to defeat decisively, to strike ❶

The team got **clobbered** seven to zip.

I'll **clobber** you if you don't <u>shut up</u>.

see also: CREAM, CRUSH, KICK ONE'S ASS, LICK, MASSACRE, SLAUGHTER

## close call [klous kɔ́ːl] *n* a narrow escape ❶

The bullet missed his heart by an inch. It was a <u>real</u> **close call**. He nearly died.

## clout [klaut] *n* power, influence ❶

Everybody listens to what he says because he's got a lot of **clout**.

see also: PULL

## clown around [klaun aráund] *v* to play ❶

<u>OK</u> kids, stop **clowning around**. It's time for bed.

see also: FOOL AROUND, HORSE AROUND

## clunk [klʌŋk] *n* the sound of a blow ❶

The bowling ball went **"clunk"** when he dropped it on the floor.

see also: BAM, BOOM, KABOOM, WHAM

## clunker [klʌŋkər] *n* an old vehicle ❶

My car's an old **clunker**, but it still runs.

see also: HEAP, JALOPY

## "c'mon" [kəmáːn] *inter* [from *come on*] used to plead ❶ or challenge

**C'mon**! The <u>cops</u> are coming! Let's go! Hurry up! **C'mon** <u>already</u>!

**C'mon** John, don't get so angry.

**C'mon**! There's no way your team will beat ours!

**coast** [koust] *v* to move easily and without effort, to ❸
relax

We **coasted** up to the stoplight.

We smoked <u>pot</u> and then **coasted** for a while on the
beach.

    see also: CRUISE

**cock** [kɑk] *n* penis ❺

He says he's got a huge **cock**.

    see also: DICK, JOHNSON, PECKER, PRICK, WEENIE, WILLY

**cockamamie** [kɑkəmèimiː] *adj* crazy, foolish ❶

I've never heard such a **cockamamie** plan.

    see also: HAREBRAINED

**cocksucker** [kɑ́ksʌkər] *n* contemptible person ❺

That guy's a <u>total</u> **cocksucker**. I told you if you do
business with him he'd <u>screw you over</u>.

    see also: ASSHOLE, BASTARD, CREEP, DICK, DICKWEED, DIP,
             DIPSHIT, DOUCHE BAG, FUCK, FUCKER, JERK,
             MOTHERFUCKER, PRICK, SCHMUCK, SOB, SON OF A BITCH

**cockteaser** [kɑ́ktiːzər] *n* a woman who leads a man ❺
on sexually, but refuses to copulate

At first I thought she was interested in me, but when I
saw her acting <u>horny</u> around all the guys I realized she
was just a **cockteaser**.

**cocky** [kɑ́kiː] *adj* arrogant, annoyingly self-assured ❶

He acts like he's a famous movie star. He <u>really</u> is
**cocky**.

Tom is one **cocky** <u>bastard</u>.

    see also: ATTITUDE, HIGHFALUTIN', SNOOTY, SNOTTY, STUCK UP,
             UPPITY

**coed** [kouéd] *adj* [from *coeducational*] something ❶
used by both sexes

This dorm is **coed**.

**coed** [kouéd] n [from *coeducational*] a young college ❶
woman

The professor dumped his wife for a **coed**.

**coke** [kouk] *n* [from *cocaine*] ❸

The robbers were all high on **coke** during the bank
heist.

**cold** [kould] *adj* unfriendly, uninterested ❶

A: Why were you so **cold** to me?

B: I wasn't acting **cold** to you, I was just feelin' kind of
out of it.

A: Yeah, right. You were ignoring me so that other girls
wouldn't think I was your girlfriend!

**cold-blooded** [kould blʌ́did] *adj* cruel, indifferent ❶
to the suffering of others

He's a **cold-blooded** person, so he ought to do real well
in Hollywood.

**cold facts** [kould fǽkts] *n* the plain truth ❶

A: It's not that I don't love you. I do. It's just that...

B: I don't want to hear a long story, OK? Just give me
the **cold facts**.

**cold feet** [kould fíːt] *n* doubts, loss of one's nerve ❶

He said he was gonna ask his wife for a divorce, but he
got **cold feet** and didn't ask her.

What's the matter? Do you have **cold feet**? I thought
you were going to join the army and go and fight in the
war.

See also: BACKOUT, CHICKEN OUT, WIMP OUT

**cold shoulder** [kould ʃóuldər] n indifferent ❶
treatment

I went to Karen's party even though she didn't invite
me and she gave me the **cold shoulder** all night. She's
been ignoring me ever since we broke up.

see also: SILENT TREATMENT

**combo** [kámbou] n [from *combination*] ❶

Rather than order a hamburger and fries separately, I'll
just get the **combo**.

I think having parents from different countries is a
good **combo**.

**"come again?"** [kʌm əgén] *inter* "What did you say?" ❶

A: You are a real jerk.

B: **Come again**? It's so noisy in here!

A: I said, YOU ARE A REAL JERK!

**come down on someone** [kʌm dáun ɑn
sʌ́mwʌn] v to criticize, severely reprimand ❶

When his father found out he had lied to him he **came
down on him** really hard and said he could never use
the car again.

see also: BAWL SOMEONE OUT, CHEW SOMEONE OUT, JUMP ALL
OVER, JUMP ON, LET SOMEONE HAVE IT, RAG ON, TAKE
IT OUT ON

**"come off it!"** [kʌm ɔ́ːf it] *inter* "Stop acting or ❹
speaking foolishly!"

**Come off it!** I can't believe you really believe in ghosts
at your age.

see also: YEAH RIGHT, VERY FUNNY

**come-on** [kʌm ɔn] *n* a phrase for attracting sexual ❶
partners

He always uses the same **come-on**: "You're the most
beautiful woman I have ever seen."

see also: PICK-UP LINE

**come on to** [kʌm ántuː] *v* to try to pick up, to flirt ❶

A: What did Larry do to Susan? Why was she crying?

B: He was drunk and was **coming on to** her pretty
strongly. I think he scared her.

see also: HIT ON

**come out of the closet** [kʌm audəv ðə klázit]
*v* to reveal one's homosexuality ❶

I've known for years that he is gay, but he just **came
out of the closet** last year.

**come through** [kʌm θruː] *v* to do what is required ❶
or anticipated

I knew you would **come through** for me <u>man</u>. Thanks
for bringing the <u>dough</u> over.

**comfy** [kʌmfiː] *adj* [from *comfortable*] comfortable ❶

I like sleeping on a water bed. It's so **comfy**

see also: COZY, CUSHY

**con** [kɑn] *v* to deceive ❶

Reagan **conned** America into believing that you can cut
taxes, increase defense spending, and everybody will
get rich. Instead the rich got richer and the poor got
poorer.

see also: BULLSHIT, SWEET TALK

**conk out** [kɑŋk áut] *v* to stop functioning  ❶

The engine **conked out** on me in the middle of the highway and I had to call a tow truck.

**conk out** [kɑŋk áut] *v* to fall asleep suddenly  ❶

We played cards last night until Sheila got sleepy and **conked out**.

see also:  CATCH SOME Z'S, SNOOZE

**con man** [kán mæn] *n* [from *confidence man*] one  ❶
who steals through deception or trickery

She completely trusted some **con man** and invested her life savings in a bank that did not exist.

see also:  CON

**connect** [kənékt] *v* to establish a rapport  ❶

A: We <u>really</u> **connect** in a lot of ways.
B: Hey, you're <u>really</u> lucky, <u>cuz</u> as far as I'm concerned, that feeling of **connection** is the same thing as love.

see also:  BOND, CLICK

**conniption fit** [kənípʃin fit] *n* a tantrum  ❶

When he found cat <u>shit</u> in his bed he had a **conniption fit** and nearly killed the cat.

see also:  FIT

**cook up** [kuk áp] *v* to concoct  ❶

He **cooked up** a scheme to make himself a millionaire.

**cool** [ku:l] *adj* under control, unemotional, lacking  ❸
in warmth

That <u>guy's</u> <u>really</u> **cool**. He doesn't talk much, but all the girls love him.

Ever since we broke up she's been <u>really</u> **cool** to me. She acts like I don't even exist.

**cool** [kuːl] *adj* good, good-looking, stylish,    ❸

Your car looks <u>really</u> **cool**.

see also:   NEAT, SLICK

**"cool it!"** [kúːl it] *imp* "Calm down!" "Relax!"    ❹

Hey, **cool it!** I want you kids to stop <u>horsing around</u> on the bed and go to sleep <u>already</u>. It's way past your bedtime.

see also:   CHILL OUT, COOL OUT

**"cool out!"** [kuːl áut] *imp* "Calm down!" "Relax!"    ❸

**Cool out** <u>man</u>! You're making too much noise.

see also:   CHILL OUT, COOL IT

**cooped up** [kuːpt ʌp] *adj* confined    ❸

I feel all **cooped up** inside during the winter

**cop** [kɑp] *n* a police officer    ❸

A **cop** pulled me over and told me I'd been speeding.

see also:   FUZZ, PIG

**cope** [koup] *v* to manage    ❶

He just couldn't **cope** with reality and had a nervous <u>breakdown</u>.

see also:   DEAL WITH, GET BY, MAKE OUT

**cop out** [kɑp áut] *v* to give up, avoid or neglect    ❶
problems

He needs to find a job so he can feed his kids. He says there aren't any jobs. But I think he's **copping out**. He just has to look harder.

see also:   BACK OUT, BAG IT, BLOW OFF, CHICKEN OUT, COLD FEET, DITCH, WALK OUT ON, WIMP OUT

**cop-out** [káp aut] *n* an inadequate excuse  ❶

Don't tell me that you're too old to be hired. That's just a **cop-out**. If you look for a job hard enough, you'll be able to find something.

**copycat** [kápi: kæt] *n* imitator  ❷

You're such a **copycat**! Why do you have to do everything I do?

**corny** [kɔ́:rni:] *adj* old-fashioned, out of style, in poor  ❶
taste

My dad's jokes are <u>really</u> **corny**. I'm sure you've heard them all a million times before. Don't laugh just to be polite or he'll go on forever.

I love old movies. I don't care if they're **corny**. They make me cry.

> see also: CHEESY

**couch potato** [káutʃ pətèitou] *n* a lazy or inactive  ❶
person, one who spends an excessive amount of time watching TV

My dad watches TV from the time he gets home from work until he goes to bed. He's a <u>total</u> **couch potato**.

**cough up** [kɔf ʌp] *v* to hand over, relinquish  ❶

He didn't want to pay me back, but he **coughed up** the <u>dough</u> after I threatened to tell his boss.

**couldn't care less** [kúdənt kɛər les] *exp* to be  ❶
completely indifferent

A: I know you dislike him, but he's dying.

B: **I couldn't care less**. Let him die. I'm not donating one of my kidneys.

**count on** [kaunt ɔn] *v* to depend on ❶

Don't be late, <u>OK</u>? I'm **counting on** you to help me move.

**country bumpkin** [kʌntriː bʌ́mpkin] *n* an ❶ unsophisticated person, or person from a rural area

He's such a **country bumpkin**. He trusts everybody.

see also: HICK

**cover** [kʌ́vər] *v* to provide protection, often with ❶ gunfire

I'm going in. **Cover** me!

**cover for** [kʌ́vər fər] *v* to substitute for someone or ❶ act on their behalf

I'm feeling pretty sick today. Can someone **cover for** me?

**cover-up** [kʌ́vər ʌ̀p] *n* a concealment of an illegal or ❶ unethical situation or activity

The mayor's office admitted to a **cover-up** of evidence that the mayor's staff had been taking bribes.

**cover up** [kʌ̀vər ʌ́p] *v* to hide evidence ❶

The government **covered up** the truth.

**cozy** [kóuziː] *adj* comfortable and warm ❶

I wouldn't say I'm in love with her, but we have a real **cozy** relationship. We've known each other for years.

I love reading by the fireplace when it's cold outside. It's so **cozy**.

see also: COMFY

**crabby** [krǽbiː] *adj* irritable ❶

You have no friends because you act like a **crabby** old man.

see also: GROUCHY

**crack up** [kræk ʌp] *v* to burst our laughing ❶

When he heard the joke he **cracked up**.

**cram** [kræm] *v* to intensely study shortly before an ❸ exam

The exam's tomorrow. I'll have to **cram** all night.

**crank** [kræŋk] *v* a bad-tempered person ❶

He's a <u>real</u> **crank**. He's always in a bad mood.

see also: GROUCH, SOURPUSS

**crank** [kræŋk] *n* to work extra hard ❶

If we **crank**, we can probably finish all the work before midnight.

see also: BREAK ONE'S BALLS, BUST ONE'S BALLS, BUST ONE'S BUTT, HUSTLE

**crap** [kræp] *v* to defecate ❹

He **crapped** under a tree during our camping trip.

see also: DUMP, POO, POOP, SHIT

**crap** [kræp] *n* excrement ❹

I stepped in dog **crap**.

see also: DOO-DOO, DUMP, POO, POOP, SHIT, TURD

**crap** [kræp] *n* nonsense ❹

Stop lying to me! I'm sick and tired of your **crap**! If you don't start talking <u>straight</u> to me I'm leaving.

He's lying. His excuse is a load of **crap**.

> see also: BALONEY, BULLSHIT, FULL OF IT, GARBAGE, JIVE, RUBBISH, TRASH

**crappy** [krǽpi:] *adj* lousy, inferior in quality ❹

That's the **crappiest** book I've ever read.

> see also: CRUMMY, FOUL, LAME, LOUSY, SHITTY

**crash** [kræʃ] *v* to go to bed or fall asleep ❸

Can I **crash** at your place tonight?

**crash** [kræʃ] *v* to go to a party uninvited ❸

She's been pissed off at me ever since I **crashed** her party.

**crash and burn** [kræʃənbɜ́rn] *v* to fail utterly ❸

A: How did your speech go?

B: It was a tough audience. I **crashed and burned**.

> see also: GO DOWN THE TUBES

**crawling with** [krɔ́:liŋ wiθ] *adj* to be infested with ❶

This neighborhood is **crawling with** criminals.

**crazy about (to be)** [tu: bi: kréizi: əbàut] *v* in love ❶
with, infatuated with, attracted to

She's **crazy about** him

He's **crazy about** his new car.

> see also: MAD ABOUT

**crazy-ass** [krézi: æs] *adj* extreme, outrageous ❸

He's got this **crazy-ass** engine in his car that can make it go 150 miles an hour.

> see also: AWESOME, BAD, BADASS, EXCELLENT, INTENSE, OUT OF SIGHT, OUT OF THIS WORLD, RAD, SUPER, TO DIE FOR, WILD

**cream** [kri:m] *v* to defeat decisively ❶

We **creamed** the other team seven to <u>zip</u>.

see also: CLOBBER, CRUSH, KICK ONE'S ASS, LICK, MASSACRE, SLAUGHTER

**creep** [kri:p] *n* a despicable person ❶

The guy's a <u>total</u> **creep**. You can't trust him.

see also: ASSHOLE, BASTARD, COCKSUCKER, DICK, DICKWEED, DIP, DIPSHIT, DOUCHE BAG, FUCK, FUCKER, JERK, MOTHERFUCKER, PRICK, SCHMUCK, SOB, SON OF A BITCH

**creeps (the)** [ðə krí:ps] *n* feelings of horror or ❶ repugnance

He gives me **the creeps**. He seems like the type that would be a child molester.

see also: WILLIES

**creepy** [krí:pi:] *adj* scary and uncomfortable ❶

This house is **creepy**. Let's get out of here.

see also: SPOOKY

**cretin** [krí:tin] *n* a stupid person ❶

The guy is a **cretin**. You can't expect him to know the answer.

see also: AIRHEAD, BIRDBRAIN, BLOCKHEAD, BONEHEAD, BOZO, DIMWIT, DINGBAT, DITZ, DODO, DOPE, DUMBELL, DUMMY, GOOF, GOOFBALL, KNUCKLEHEAD, LAMEBRAIN, MEATHEAD, NINCOMPOOP, NUMBSKULL, PEA-BRAIN, RETARD, SCATTERBRAIN, SPACE CADET, TWIT

**croak** [krouk] *v* to die ❷

His dog **croaked** because it ate too much.

see also: KEEL OVER

**crook** [kruk] *n* person who engages in fraudulent or criminal practices ❶

If I find the **crook** who stole my car I'll beat the <u>shit</u> out of him.

**crud** [krʌd] *n* dirty, worthless matter ❶

There's some sort of **crud** stuck to my shoe.

see also: GUNK

**cruddy** [krʌdiː] *adj* dirty, in bad condition ❶

Don't put your **cruddy** boots on the furniture!

see also: DINGY, GNARLY, GRODY, GROSS, ICKY, YUCKY

**cruise** [kruːz] *v* to drive or move smoothly and effortlessly ❸

A: We were **cruising** around LA looking for a place to sleep.

B: Then what happened?

A: Well, we **cruised** past this beach party, and decided to <u>crash</u> it.

I'm starving. Let's **cruise** to a restaurant and grab a bite to eat.

see also: COAST

**crummy** [krʌmiː] *adj* bad, of low quality ❶

I hate this **crummy** job. I think I'm <u>gonna</u> quit.

This car's really **crummy**. I knew I shouldn't have bought it used.

see also: CRAPPY, FOUL, LAME, LOUSY, SHITTY

**crush** [krʌʃ] *n* an intense infatuation, strong feeling of love ❶

She has a **crush** on the captain of the football team, even though she's never talked to him.

see also: HOTS

**crush** [krʌʃ] *v* to defeat decisively ❶

The Braves **crushed** the Yankees fifteen to <u>zip</u>.

see also: CLOBBER, CREAM, KICK ONE'S ASS, LICK, MASSACRE, SLAUGHTER

**crushed** [krʌʃ] *adj* to be emotionally devastated ❶

She was **crushed** when her boyfriend left her.

**crybaby** [kráibeibiː] *n* a person who complains or cries constantly ❷

Don't be a **crybaby**. You can't complain every time someone forgets to say "thanks."

see also: BABY, WEENIE, WUSS

**cum/come** [kʌm] *v* to have an orgasm ❹

I'm **cumming**, I'm **cumming**!

A: Did you **come**?
B: Yeah, I **came**.

**cum/come** [kʌm] *n* semen ❹

Oh <u>gross</u>! Get some toilet paper. There's **cum** <u>all over the place</u>.

**cunt** [kʌnt] *n* very vulgar term for female genitals, or for a woman in general ❻

I hate it when they don't show the girls' **cunts** in porno films.

You <u>fuckin'</u> **cunt**! You cheated on me while I was in jail? I'm <u>gonna</u> <u>fuckin'</u> kill you. Did you think that I wouldn't find out?

see also: BEAVER, BITCH, PUSSY

**cushy/cush** [kuʃiː, kuʃ] *adj* [from *cushioned*] very ❸ soft and comfortable, easy

This sofa is really **cushy**.

He has a pretty **cush** lifestyle.

see also: COMFY

**cut** [kʌt] *adj* muscular, well defined ❸

Look at how **cut** that <u>guy</u> is. <u>Wow</u>! He doesn't have an ounce of fat on him.

see also: BUILT, IN SHAPE

**cut class** [kʌt klæs] *v* to skip school ❸

When I was in high school I always used to **cut** class and go to the pizza place.

**cute** [kjuːt] *adj* pretty or handsome ❸

He's the **cutest** guy in the school.

see also: GOOD-LOOKING, GORGEOUS

**cut in** [kʌt in] *v* to take a place ahead of one's proper ❶ turn

Hey, I saw you! You can't **cut in** line like that! Wait your turn like the rest of us.

He **cut in** front of that car, so the driver shot at him.

**cut it** [kʌt it] *v* to be effective or satisfactory ❶

I know he wants to be on the football team, but he just can't **cut it** this year.

**"cut it out!"** [kʌt it áut] *imp* "Stop!" "Desist!"    ❶

Why are you teasing that puppy? **Cut it out!**

**Cut it out** you guys! Stop fighting.

**cut loose** [kʌt luːs] *v* to break all ties and leave    ❶

A: What happened to Joe after he found out that his wife was cheating on him?

B: He **cut loose**, moved to another state, changed his name, and found a new wife.

see also: CLEAR OUT, SPLIT

**cutoffs** [kʌtɔfs] *n* shorts that have been made from    ❶
long pants

I was wearing a pair of **cutoffs** that I made last year.

**"cut one some slack!"** [kʌt wʌn sʌm slæk] *imp*    ❶
"Be understanding!" "Be flexible!"

A: Why don't you get a job <u>already</u>? You've been <u>hangin' around</u> here for over two weeks.

B: **Cut me some slack**, <u>OK</u>? I just got out of the <u>slammer</u>.

see also: GIMME A BREAK

**cut the cheese** [kʌt ðə tʃíːz] *v* to pass intestinal gas    ❷

Who **cut the cheese**? It stinks in here.

see also: FART, LAY A FART

**cutthroat** [kʌt θróut] *adj* ruthless    ❶

Capitalism is based on **cutthroat** competition.

see also: DOG-EAT-DOG

**cuz/cause** [kʌz] *conj* [from *because*]    ❶

I went to the store **cuz** I wanted to buy some food for dinner.

# D

**dad** [dæd] *n* father, term of address ❷

**Dad**, can I borrow the car tonight? I have a date and we <u>wanna</u> go to a movie.

see also: DADDY, OLD MAN, POP

**daddy** [dǽdiː] *n* father, term of address ❷

**Daddy**, pick me up and put me on your shoulders!

see also: DAD, POP

**"dagnabbit"/"dag"** [dægnǽbit, dæg] *inter* ❶
expression of anger, frustration or surprise

**Dag**, that <u>girl</u> is <u>hot</u>.

see also: DANG, DARN, GEE, GOLLY, GOOD GRIEF, GOSH, JEEZ

**damn** [dæm] *n* a minimum amount or degree ❹

I don't give a **damn** what the neighbors think, we're not repainting the house!

see also: FUCK

**"damn!"** [dæm] *inter* expression of annoyance, disgust ❹
or surprise

**Damn**! I locked the keys in the car.

**Damn** it! I forgot to meet her for dinner.

see also: CHRIST, FOR CHRISTSAKE, GOD, JESUS CHRIST

**damned** [dæmd] *adj* added to express annoyance, ❹
disgust or anger

I locked the **damned** keys in the **damned** car.

see also: DOGGONED, FREAKIN, FRICKIN, FRIGGIN, FUCKING

**"dang!"/"darn!"** [dæŋ, dɑrn] *inter* expression of ❶
annoyance, disgust or surprise

**Dang**. I forgot to bring a condom.

> see also: DAG, DRAT, GEE, GOLLY, GOOD GRIEF, GOSH, JEEZ,
> RATS, SHOOT

**dead** [ded] *adj* in big trouble ❸

You're **dead** <u>motherfucker</u>. I'm <u>gonna</u> kill you.

> see also: DONE FOR, FUCKED, SCREWED

**dead** [ded] *adj* very tired ❶

I feel **dead**. I think I'll go to bed.

> see also: BEAT, BLEARY-EYED, BURNED OUT, BUSHED, FRAZZLED,
> FRIED, OUT OF IT, POOPED, WASTED, WIPED OUT,
> ZONKED OUT

**deadbeat** [dédbiːt] *n* lazy, irresponsible person ❶

That guy's a <u>real</u> **deadbeat**. He left his wife and kids
and never sends them any money.

**deadbeat** [dédbiːt] *adj* lazy or irresponsible ❶

The government is trying to make **deadbeat** dads pay
their alimony.

**deal** [diːl] *v* to sell drugs ❶

He's been **dealing** drugs ever since he was a teenager.

**deal** [diːl] *n* a transaction or arrangement ❶

The salesman will give you a better **deal** if you mention
my name.

**deal with** [diːl wiθ] *v* handle or manage ❶

I can't **deal with** her <u>attitude</u>. She's such a <u>bitch</u>.

> see also: COPE, GET BY, MAKE OUT

**decent** [díːsint] *adj* respectable, passable, acceptable  ❶

Portland is a pretty **decent** place. I think I could live there.

Three hundred dollars is a **decent** price for that tape recorder.

**decked out** [dekt áut] *adj* decorated, fancily dressed  ❶

A: Wow, you're all **decked out**! Where did you get those clothes?

B: We just rented these tuxes for a friend's wedding, that's all.

see also: SPIFFED UP, SPIFFY

**dibs** [dibz] *n* first claim on something  ❸

I've got **dibs** on this seat. If you take it, I'll be pissed.

**dicey** [daisiː] *adj* unstable or unpredictable  ❶

The racial situation in America is pretty **dicey**. It could blow at any time.

see also: IFFY

**dick** [dik] *n* penis  ❺

He's always scratching his **dick**.

see also: COCK, JOHNSON, PECKER, PRICK, WEENIE, WILLY

**dick** [dik] *n* a despicable person  ❺

That guy's a real **dick**. He said he would meet me here at seven o'clock and it's already ten.

see also: ASSHOLE, BASTARD, COCKSUCKER, CREEP, DICKWEED, DIP, DIPSHIT, DOUCHE BAG, FUCK, FUCKER, JERK, MOTHERFUCKER, PRICK, SCHMUCK, SOB, SON OF A BITCH

## dick [dik] *n* nothing ❺

You won't get **dick** from me after the way you <u>ripped</u> me <u>off</u>.

see also: DIDDLY, JACK SHIT, PEANUTS, SQUAT, ZILCH, ZIP

## dick (one) around [dik wʌn əráund] *v* to mistreat, ❺ to fool around

Stop **dicking me around** <u>man</u>. If you don't stop <u>ripping</u> me <u>off</u> I'll call the <u>cops</u>.

see also: FUCK WITH, MESS WITH

## dickweed [díkwi:d] *n* a despicable person ❺

He's a <u>real</u> **dickweed**. He only thinks of himself.

see also: ASSHOLE, BASTARD, COCKSUCKER, CREEP, DICK, DIP, DIPSHIT, DOUCHE BAG, FUCK, FUCKER, JERK, MOTHERFUCKER, PRICK, SCHMUCK, SOB, SON OF A BITCH

## diddly (squat) [dídli: skwɑt] *n* a pittance, nothing ❸

He never gave me **diddlysquat**.

There's nothing here. I don't see **diddly**.

see also: DICK, JACK SHIT, PEANUTS, SQUAT, ZILCH, ZIP

## dig [dig] *v* to appreciate, understand ❸

I <u>really</u> **dig** these shoes.

see also: INTO

## "dig in!" [dig in] *inter* "Eat heartily!" ❶

<u>OK</u> everybody, the food's ready. **Dig in!**

## dillydally [díli: dæli:] *v* to procrastinate, dawdle ❶

Hurry up <u>already</u> will <u>ya</u>! Why do you always have to **dillydally**? If we don't leave now we'll be late.

**dimwit** [dímwit] *n* a stupid person ❶

He's a bit of a **dimwit**. He always asks dumb questions.

see also: AIRHEAD, BIRDBRAIN, BLOCKHEAD, BONEHEAD, BOZO, CRETIN, DINGBAT, DITZ, DODO, DOPE, DUMBELL, DUMMY, GOOF, GOOFBALL, KNUCKLEHEAD, LAMEBRAIN, MEATHEAD, NINCOMPOOP, NUMBSKULL, PEA-BRAIN, RETARD, SCATTERBRAIN, SPACE CADET, TWIT

**din-din** [din din] *n* [from *dinner*] ❷

Come here Rover, it's time for **din-din**.

**dingbat** [díŋbæt] *n* a forgetful or unaware person ❶

She's such a **dingbat**. She always forgets to lock her house.

see also: AIRHEAD, BIRDBRAIN, BLOCKHEAD, BONEHEAD, BOZO, CRETIN, DIMWIT, DITZ, DODO, DOPE, DUMBELL, DUMMY, GOOF, GOOFBALL, KNUCKLEHEAD, LAMEBRAIN, MEATHEAD, NINCOMPOOP, NUMBSKULL, PEA-BRAIN, RETARD, SCATTERBRAIN, SPACE CADET, TWIT

**dingy** [díndʒiː] *adj* dirty, discolored ❶

Let's throw out this **dingy** carpet.

see also: CRUDDY, GNARLY, GRODY, GROSS, ICKY, YUCKY

**dinky** [díŋkiː] *adj* small ❸

A: Why did you refuse to marry him? I thought you were crazy about him.

B: The engagement ring he gave me must have been cheap. It had the **dinkiest** diamond I'd ever seen.

see also: MICKEY MOUSE, RINKY-DINK

**dip/dipshit** [dip, dípʃit] *n* a stupid or ❶ ❹
unsophisticated person

He's such a **dipshit**. He says things just to bother people.

see also: ASSHOLE, BASTARD, COCKSUCKER, CREEP, DICK, DICKWEED, DOUCHE BAG, FUCK, FUCKER, JERK, MOTHERFUCKER, PRICK, SCHMUCK, SOB, SON OF A BITCH

**dirtbag/dirtball** [dərtbæg, dərtbɔːl] *n* a dirty or    ❸
disgusting person

I hate that **dirtbag**. He stole my <u>girl</u>.

see also:  SCUMBAG, SLEAZE, SLEAZEBAG, SLIMEBUCKET

**dirt cheap** [dərt tʃiːp] *adj* very inexpensive    ❶

I bought two televisions '<u>cuz</u> they were **dirt cheap**.

see also:  STEAL

**dirty** [dɜ́rdiː] *adj* vulgar, indecent    ❶

He's got a **dirty** mouth.

see also:  SLEAZY

**dirty** [dɜ́rdiː] *adv* unfairly, deceptively

He plays **dirty**.

**dis** [dis] *v* [from *disrespect*] to have disrespect for    ❸

You <u>gonna</u> let him **dis** you like that? You should stand
up for yourself.

see also:  FLAME, TRASH

**disappearing act** [disəpíəriŋ ækt] *n* to vanish    ❶

A: What happened to her boyfriend after all her money
was stolen?

B: He pulled a **disappearing act**. No one could figure
out where he went.

A: You think he's the one who stole it?

B: No doubt about it.

**discombobulated** [diskʌmbábjuːlèidid] *adj*    ❶
confused, disorganized

Lou was pretty **discombobulated** after he fell on his
head.

**ditch** [ditʃ] *v* to abandon, to dispose of ❶

I think I'm gonna **ditch** this car soon. It's already twenty years old.

see also: BACK OUT, BAG IT, BLOW OFF, CHICKEN OUT, COLD FEET, COP OUT, WALK OUT ON, WIMP OUT

**ditz** [dits] *n* a silly or foolish person ❶

That girl sure is a **ditz**. She called her new boyfriend by her old boyfriend's name.

see also: AIRHEAD, BIRDBRAIN, BLOCKHEAD, BONEHEAD, BOZO, CRETIN, DIMWIT, DINGBAT, DODO, DOPE, DUMBELL, DUMMY, GOOF, GOOFBALL, KNUCKLEHEAD, LAMEBRAIN, MEATHEAD, NINCOMPOOP, NUMBSKULL, PEA-BRAIN, RETARD, SCATTERBRAIN, SPACE CADET, TWIT

**ditzy** [ditsiː] *adj* stupid, foolish ❶

She's so **ditzy**, she forgets her own name sometimes.

see also: NOT TOO SWIFT, RETARDED

**divvy** [diviː] *v* [from *divide*] to divide or share ❶

After my uncle died we **divvied** up his property.

see also: SPLIT

**dodo** [dóudou] *n* stupid or foolish person ❶

You're looking for your glasses? You're such a **dodo**. They're on top of your head!

see also: AIRHEAD, BIRDBRAIN, BLOCKHEAD, BONEHEAD, BOZO, CRETIN, DIMWIT, DINGBAT, DITZ, DOPE, DUMBELL, DUMMY, GOOF, GOOFBALL, KNUCKLEHEAD, LAMEBRAIN, MEATHEAD, NINCOMPOOP, NUMBSKULL, PEA-BRAIN, RETARD, SCATTERBRAIN, SPACE CADET, TWIT

**dog** [dɔːg] *n* an ugly girl or woman ❹

Danny's new girlfriend is a <u>real</u> **dog**, but they say she's nice.

**dog** [dɔːg] *n* a sexually promiscuous man ❸

Danny's a <u>real</u> **dog**. He sleeps with a different girl every night.

see also: ANIMAL, SLUT

**dog-eat-dog** [dɔːg ɪːt dɔːg] *adj* ruthless ❸

You'd better watch out when you're in LA. It's a **dog-eat-dog** world out there.

see also: CUTTHROAT

**doggie style** [dɔ́ːgiː staɪl] *adv* having sex from the ❺
rear

He loves doing it **doggie style**.

**doggoned** [dɔ́ːgɑnd] *int* added to express annoyance, ❶
disgust or surprise

Get your **doggoned** car out of my driveway.

see also: DAMNED, FREAKIN, FRICKIN, FRIGGIN, FUCKING

**done deal** [dʌn díːl] *n* a finished transaction ❶

Hey, you can't return these drugs. Once you buy them, that's it. It's a **done deal**.

**done for** [dʌn fɔr] *adj* exhausted, worn out ❶

We're **done for**. We're out of <u>ammo</u> and the enemy is closing in.

see also: DEAD, FUCKED, SCREWED

**Don Juan** [dɑn wán] *n* a man who seduces many ❶
women for sex, a Casanova

She always gets hurt in relationships, but it's her own <u>damned</u> fault. She really likes those **Don Juan** types.

see also: LADY'S MAN, WOMANIZER

**don't give a damn/fuck** [dount giv ə dǽm, fʌk] ❺
v not to care in the least

I **don't give a fuck** about his feelings, he's a murderer.

see also: DON'T GIVE A SHIT

**don't give a shit** [dount giv ə ʃit] v not to care in ❺
the least

I **don't give a shit** what anybody thinks. I'm going to
dye my hair green.

see also: DON'T GIVE A DAMN/FUCK

**doo-doo** [dú: du:] n excrement ❷

Mike stepped in a pile of dog **doo-doo**!

If we don't get this work completed on time we're going
to be in deep **doo-doo**.

see also: CRAP, POO, POOP, SHIT, TURD

**doohickey** [dú:hiki:] n a small device or article ❶

A: Why was that kid's mom so upset?

B: Her kid was playing with some little **doohickey**, and
then nearly choked on the <u>damned</u> thing.

see also: GIZMO, THINGAMAJIG, WHATCHAMACALLIT

**doozy** [dú:zi:] n, adj an extraordinary one of its kind ❶

Watch your step. The first one is a **doozy**.

I had a **doozy** of a time trying to read his handwriting.

see also: ZINGER

## dope [doup] *n* a silly or foolish person ❶

Tommy's a real **dope**. I asked him to go to the store and buy beer and he came back with orange juice. Can you believe it?

see also: AIRHEAD, BIRDBRAIN, BLOCKHEAD, BONEHEAD, BOZO, CRETIN, DIMWIT, DINGBAT, DITZ, DODO, DUMBELL, DUMMY, GOOF, GOOFBALL, KNUCKLEHEAD, LAMEBRAIN, MEATHEAD, NINCOMPOOP, NUMBSKULL, PEA-BRAIN, RETARD, SCATTERBRAIN, SPACE CADET, TWIT

## dope [doup] *n* narcotics, illegal drugs ❶

I've got any kinda **dope** you need, <u>man</u>. You need heroin, I've got it. Need cocaine? I've got that too.

see also: GRASS, HASH, POT, WEED

## dope fiend [doup fiːnd] *n* a drug addict ❸

A: What's his problem? Why can't he get a job and stop living in the street?

B: That boy's a <u>real</u> **dope fiend**. He spends every cent he's got on <u>coke</u>.

see also: JUNKIE

## dork [dɔrk] *n* a stupid, unfashionable person ❸

He looks like a **dork**, but he's actually a very good athlete.

see also: DRIP, DWEEB, GEEK, NERD

## dorky [dɔ́rkiː] *adj* stupid-looking, unfashionable ❸

Why does she always have to wear such **dorky** dresses?

## double-cross [dʌbl krɔ́ːs] *v* to betray ❶

The spy was **double-crossed** by his beautiful girlfriend. He didn't know it but she was a spy too.

see also: STAB IN THE BACK

**douche bag** [dúːʃ bæg] *n* a despicable person ❺

There's the **douche bag** who stole my Walkman while I was sleeping!

see also: ASSHOLE, BASTARD, COCKSUCKER, CREEP, DICK, DICKWEED, DIP, DIPSHIT, FUCK, FUCKER, JERK, MOTHERFUCKER, PRICK, SCHMUCK, SOB, SON OF A BITCH

**dough** [dou] *n* money ❸

I'm out of **dough**. Could you lend me a little?

see also: BREAD, MOOLA

**do up** [duː ʌp] *v* to make attractive, glamorous or fancy ❶

I **did up** my hair and wore my new gown to the ball.

**down** [daun] *adj* depressed ❸

She's been **down** about this for weeks.

He's been feeling **down** ever since his girlfriend left him for his best friend.

see also: BLAHS, BLUES, BUMMED, BUMMED OUT, FUNK

**downer** [dáunər] *n* a depressing event or situation ❸

That's a <u>real</u> **downer**. I'm sorry to hear about her father's death.

see also: BUMMER, DRAG, PITS

**downside** [dáun said] *n* the negative aspect ❶

A woman to her husband: "The <u>up side</u> is that I'm pregnant. The **downside** is that it is not your baby."

see also: CATCH, FLIP SIDE, SMALL PRINT

**down-to-earth** [daun tu: ɔ́rθ] *adj* simple, realistic, ❶
direct

Most farmers are pretty **down-to-earth** <u>folks</u>.

see also: REAL

**drag** [dræg] *n* a depressing or frustrating event or ❸
situation

You didn't pass the test? That's a **drag**. <u>Whatcha</u> <u>gonna</u>
do?

I hate traffic jams. It's such a **drag** to have to sit in a car
for hours.

see also: BUMMER, DOWNER, PITS

**"drat!"/"drats!"** [dræt, dræts] *inter* expression of ❷
annoyance, disgust or surprise

**Drat!** I thought I would win the bet, but I lost.

see also: DAG, DANG, DARN, GEE, GOLLY, GOOD GRIEF, GOSH,
JEEZ, RATS, SHOOT

**dreads/dreadlocks** [dredz, drédlɑks] *n* ropelike ❸
style of hair formed by matting or braiding

Didn't your last girlfriend have <u>real</u> long **dreads**?

**drift** [drift] *n* meaning, intention ❶

A: You get my **drift**?

B: Sorry <u>man</u>, I still don't <u>get it</u>. What exactly are you
trying to tell me?

**drip** [drip] *n* a boring or unattractive person ❶

He's a <u>real</u> **drip**. No one ever invites him to parties.

see also: DORK, DWEEB, GEEK, NERD

**"drop dead!"** [drɑp déd] *imp* a pointed insult ❹
"To hell with you!"

**Drop dead**, <u>asshole</u>!

see also: BUG OFF, GET LOST

**duck** [dʌk] *v* to lower the head or body suddenly ❶
They threw a snowball at me, but I **ducked** and it hit the guy behind me.

**dud** [dʌd] *n* something that is broken or ineffectual ❶
This lightbulb is a **dud**. It doesn't light up.

**dude** [duːd] *n* a man ❸
Who's that weird-looking **dude** over there with the hat?

see also: BUD, GUY, MAN

**dude** [duːd] *n* a term of address for a young man ❸
Hey **dude**! <u>What's up</u>?

see also: BUD, GUY, MAN

**"duh!"** [dəː] *inter* scornful acknowledgment of the ❷
obvious

A: Where are my glasses?

B: **Duh!** They're on top of your head!

**dullsville** [dʌ́lzvil] *n* boring situation or person ❸
This party is, <u>like</u>, **dullsville**, <u>man</u>. Let's get out of here.

**dumbbell** [dʌ́mbel] *n* a stupid person ❶
He's a complete **dumbbell**. He can't even add.

see also: AIRHEAD, BIRDBRAIN, BLOCKHEAD, BONEHEAD, BOZO, CRETIN, DIMWIT, DINGBAT, DITZ, DODO, DOPE, DUMMY, GOOF, GOOFBALL, KNUCKLEHEAD, LAMEBRAIN, MEATHEAD, NINCOMPOOP, NUMBSKULL, PEA-BRAIN, RETARD, SCATTERBRAIN, SPACE CADET, TWIT

**dummy** [dʌ́mi:] *n* a stupid person ❶

You **dummy**! I can't believe how much of a <u>dodo</u> you are sometimes. You're about to brush your teeth with haircream!

see also: AIRHEAD, BIRDBRAIN, BLOCKHEAD, BONEHEAD, BOZO, CRETIN, DIMWIT, DINGBAT, DITZ, DODO, DOPE, DUMBELL, GOOF, GOOFBALL, KNUCKLEHEAD, LAMEBRAIN, MEATHEAD, NINCOMPOOP, NUMBSKULL, PEA-BRAIN, RETARD, SCATTERBRAIN, SPACE CADET, TWIT

**dump** [dʌmp] *n* an objectionable place ❶

This place is a <u>real</u> **dump**, but at least it's cheap.

see also: SHITHOLE

**dump** [dʌmp] *n, v* defecation ❹

Where's the bathroom? I <u>gotta</u> take a **dump**.

see also: CRAP, DOO-DOO, POO, POOP, SHIT, TURD

**dump** [dʌmp] *v* to leave a lover ❸

She **dumped** me like I meant nothing to her.

**dweeb** [dwi:b] *n* an unfashionable person ❸

I would never date a <u>guy</u> like that. He's such a **dweeb**.

see also: DORK, DRIP, GEEK, NERD

**dying to** [dáiŋ tu:] *v* to long for desperately ❶

I'm **dying to** go to Hawaii.

**dyke** [daik] *n* offensive term for a lesbian ❹

She acts so <u>butch</u>, I bet she's a **dyke**.

see also: BUTCH

**"dynamite!"** [dáinəmait] *inter* "Wonderful!" ❸
"Fantastic!"

You got a perfect score on the test? **Dynamite**! I'm so happy for you!

see also: AWESOME, EXCELLENT, FAR OUT, GREAT, OUT OF SIGHT, RIGHT ON, WOW

# E

**earful** [íərful] *n* a lot of information or gossip, a ❶ scolding

She loves to gossip. She gave me an **earful**.

**easy ride** [ì:zi: ráid] *n* a woman who is free with sex ❸

A: Why's everybody so interested in Claudia? She <u>ain't</u> even pretty.

B: Because she's an **easy ride**.

see also: BIMBO, HUSSY, NYMPHO, SLUT

**eat it up** [i:didʌp] *v* to enjoy greatly ❶

They were complimenting him and he was **eating it up**.

**edge** [edʒ] *n* a penetrating or harsh quality ❶

I love Nirvana's lyrics and music. They have a <u>real</u> **edge** to them.

**egg someone on** [èg sʌmwʌn á:n] *v* to encourage ❶ or provoke someone

There was a kid threatening to jump off the building, and some idiotic people were actually **egging him on**.

**elbow grease** [élbou griːs] *n* hard work and effort  ❶

You'll pass the bar exam, but it's going to take some **elbow grease**.

**'em** [əm] *contr* [from *him* or *them*]  ❶

I saw **'em** down by the river.

**'er** [ər] *contr* [from *her*]  ❶

I saw **'er** yesterday.

**'ere** [iər] *contr* [from *here*]  ❶

Come **'ere** <u>an'</u> talk to me.

**every which way** [evəriː wítʃ wei] *adv* in every direction  ❶

People were running **every which way** when the fire started.

    see also:  ALL OVER, HERE AND THERE

**evil eye** [ìːvul ái] *n* an angry stare  ❶

He gave me the **evil eye** because he thought I was <u>hitting on</u> his girlfriend.

**ex** [eks] *n* [from *ex-husband* or *ex-wife*]  ❶

My **ex** got remarried last year.

**exam** [igzǽm, egzǽm] *n* [from *examination*]  ❶

I've got an **exam** tomorrow, so let me study, <u>OK</u>?

**excellent** [éksəlent] *adj* wonderful  ❸

She's got this **excellent** new boyfriend, and his car is <u>like</u>, <u>really</u> **excellent**.

    see also:  AWESOME, BAD, BADASS, CRAZY-ASS, INTENSE, OUT OF SIGHT, OUT OF THIS WORLD, RAD, SUPER, TO DIE FOR, WILD

**"excellent!"** [éksəlent] *inter* "Wonderful!"  ❸

A: The Yankees won!

B: That's **excellent**!

see also: AWESOME, DYNAMITE, FAR OUT, GREAT, OUT OF SIGHT, RIGHT ON, WOW

**eyeball** [áibɔːl] *v* to observe intently  ❶

He **eyeballs** every girl who walks by.

see also: CHECK OUT, SCOPE

# F

**fag/faggot** [fæg, fǽgət] *n* very offensive term for a  ❺
male homosexual

I'll bet he's a **fag**.

see also: FAIRY, FLAMER, QUEEN, QUEER

**fairy** [féəriː] *n* offensive term for a male homosexual  ❹

Have you seen the way that guy walks? I'll bet he's a **fairy**.

see also: FAG, FLAMER, QUEEN, QUEER

**fake** [feik] *adj* insincere  ❶

He's one of those **fake** people who pretend to be your friend when they want something.

see also: BOGUS, PHONY

**fake it** [féik it] *v* to pretend  ❶

She doesn't enjoy sex that much. She just **fakes it** to make her boyfriend happy.

see also: MAKE LIKE

**fake out** [feik áut] v to deceive ❶
The crook **faked out** the <u>cops</u> by wearing a disguise.

**fall for** [fɔ:l fər] v to be deceived or swindled ❶
A: How did the robber get into the house?
B: He told me he was a salesman, so I let him in.
A: I can't believe you **fell for** that.

**falling out** [fɔ:liŋ áut] n a disagreement or quarrel ❶
They used to be <u>totally</u> in love, but recently had a **falling out**. Now they don't even talk to each other.

**fall through** [fɔ:l θrú:] v to collapse or fail ❶
He was going to sell his house, but then the deal **fell through**.

**fanny** [fǽni:] n buttocks (warning: this is a British-English term for *vagina*) ❷
Get your **fanny** over here and get this homework done.
see also: ASS, BOTTOM, BUM, BUNS, BUTT, HEINIE, REAR END

**far-out** [fár aut] adj unusual or eccentric ❶
She was wearing these <u>really</u> **far-out** earrings made of fur.
see also: WAY-OUT

**"far out!"** [far áut] inter "Fantastic!" "Amazing!" ❸
**Far out!** I can't believe you're getting married! Congratulations!

**fart** [fart] n flatulence, intestinal gas ❹
Something stinks! <u>Phew</u>, did somebody cut a **fart** around here?

74

**fart** [fart] *v* to pass intestinal gas ❹

<u>Oh my God!</u> Something smells awful. Did you **fart** again?

see also: CUT THE CHEESE, LAY A FART

**fart around** [fart əràund] *v* to waste time by loitering ❹ or delaying

Why are you **farting around**? You should be doing your homework!

see also: GOOF OFF

**fast lane** [fǽst lein] *n* a free-spending and ❶ self-indulgent lifestyle

Ever since he got a job on Wall Street, he's been living in the **fast lane**, drinking, making piles of money, and dating lots of girls.

**fat chance** [fæt tʃǽns] *n* little or no possiblity ❶

He thinks I'll sleep with him? **Fat chance** that'll ever happen!

see also: NO WAY

**fatso** [fǽtsou] *n* an overweight or fat person ❷

Mommy, I don't want to go to school any more because everybody is always making fun of me and calling me "**fatso**."

see also: BLIMP, PORKER

**faze** [feiz] *v* to bother or disturb ❶

She spit in his face, but it didn't even **faze** him.

**fed up with (to be)** [tuː biː fed ʌp wiθ] *adj*  ❶
disgusted, unwilling to put up with something

I'm **fed up with** my job. My boss treats me like <u>shit</u>. I'm <u>gonna</u> quit tomorrow.

see also: SICK AND TIRED OF, SICK OF

**feel** [fiːl] *n* a natural intuition and talent  ❶

He's a gifted piano player with a <u>real</u> **feel** for the music.

**fender bender** [féndər bendər] *n* a minor car  ❶
accident

Today I crashed into the back of a bus. Luckily, it was just a **fender bender**.

**fifty-fifty** [fífdiː fífdiː] *adv* half and half, equally  ❶

Neither of us has enough money to rent this car on our own, but if we split the cost **fifty-fifty**, we can afford it.

**fight dirty** [fait dərdiː] *v* to cheat or break the rules  ❶

He **fights dirty** so watch out for him. He'll lie, cheat, and steal—whatever it takes to win.

see also: PLAY DIRTY

**figure** [fígjər] *v* to reckon, to suppose  ❶

I'm already thirty years old. I **figure** it's about time I thought about getting married.

see also: GUESS

**figure out** [figjər áut] *v* to discover or determine  ❶

I can't **figure out** what he wants from me. First, says he just wants to be friends, then he tells me how he loves me and can't live without me.

see also: CATCH ON, GET IT

**fink** [fiŋk] *n* a betrayer ❶

That guy's a **fink**. He told the teacher that we were smoking in the boy's restroom.

see also: BACKSTABBER, RAT

**fishy** [fíʃiː] *adj* suspicious ❶

He can't afford a Mercedes-Benz on his low salary. Something is **fishy**. He must be making money on the side somehow.

**fit** [fit] *n* a sudden emotional reaction ❶

My dad's going to have a **fit** when he sees how much I spent on this dress!

see also: CONNIPTION FIT

**fix** [fiks] *n* any dose of a craved drug, an intravenous injection of a narcotic ❸

I feel like shit if I don't get my morning **fix** of coffee.

The junkie was desperate for a **fix** of heroin.

**fizzle out** [fizl aut] *v* to fail, end weakly ❶

Their relationship finally **fizzled out**. They were both pursuing full-time careers, and they didn't have time for each other.

see also: PETER OUT

**flabby** [flǽbiː] *adj* fat and soft, poorly defined ❶

I haven't worked out all winter and my gut is really **flabby**. I'm gonna go on a diet tomorrow.

**flak** [flæk] *n* criticism, trouble ❶

He caught a lot of **flak** from his dad and from the police after he crashed his father's car into a tree.

I warned you that this wouldn't work, so just don't give me any **flak**.

see also: HASSLE

**flake** [fleik] *n* unreliable person, oddball ❶

I can't believe she locked herself out of her car again. She's such a **flake**.

see also: DINGBAT, DITZ, SCATTERBRAIN, SPACE CADET

**flaky** [fléikiː] *adj* absent-minded, scatterbrained ❸

You can't depend on him to pay the bills on time. He's too **flaky**.

see also: SPACEY, DITZY

**flame** [fleim] *n* a lover or sweetheart ❸

She's one of his old **flames** from college.

**flame** [fleim] *v* to criticize severely ❸

Hey <u>man</u>, you don't have to **flame** me just <u>cuz</u> I've got a different opinion than yours.

see also: DIS, TRASH

**flamer** [fléimər] *n* offensive term for a flamboyant gay ❹ man

What a **flamer**. He even walks like a woman.

see also: FAG, FAIRY, QUEEN, QUEER

**flat broke** [flæt bróuk] *adj* penniless ❶

I <u>ain't</u> got a cent to my name. I'm **flat broke**.

see also: BROKE, PISS-POOR

**flat out** [flæt áut] *int* to the greatest degree, ❶ completely

That boy is **flat out** crazy.

She **flat out** left him and took the kids.

see also: TOTALLY

**flick** [flik] *n* a movie     ❶

Let's go see a good **flick**.

**fling** [fliŋ] *n* a brief and casual sexual relationship, an ❶ affair

He went to Paris for two weeks and had a **fling** with a French girl.

see also: ONE NIGHT STAND

**flip** [flip] *adj* lacking respect     ❶

I'm sick of his **flip** <u>attitude</u>. He acts like other people don't have feelings.

**flip (out)** [flip aut] *v* to go crazy     ❶

He **flipped** when he heard that his wife was cheating on him.

When he heard his daughter was raped, he **flipped out** and tried to kill the guy who did it.

see also: BLOW A HAIRY, BLOW ONE'S COOL, FREAK, GO APESHIT, GO BANANAS, GO POSTAL, LOSE IT, LOSE ONE'S COOL

**flip side** [flip said] *n* the other side on an issue, the ❶ advantage or disadvantage

My new job is great! But the **flip side** is that the commute takes three hours.

see also: DOWNSIDE, UP SIDE

**floor** [flɔːr] *v* to press the accelerator pedal of an ❶ automobile to the floor

I **floored** it and went as fast as I could.

**floored** [flɔːrd] *adj* amazed, stunned ❶

Most people in Tokyo were **floored** when they heard about the subway attacks.

see also: BLOW AWAY

**fluke** [fluːk] *n* a very unusual occurrence, a freak ❶ occurrence

I can't believe he hit a home run. His batting average is so low that it must be a **fluke** or something.

**flunk (out)** [flʌŋk aut] *v* to fail ❸

He **flunked** the test.

He **flunked out** of high school and worked as a taxi driver before starting a successful magazine.

**folks** [fouks] *n* parents, family ❶

How are your **folks**?

My **folks** are giving me trouble about not studying enough.

**folks** [fouks] *n* people in general ❶

OK **folks**, I gotta go. See ya tomorrow.

I thought the **folks** in New York were really friendly.

**fool around** [fuːl əráund] *v* to play ❶

OK kids, stop **fooling around**! It's time for bed!

see also: HORSE AROUND, CLOWN AROUND

**fool around** [fuːl əráund] *v* to engage in casual ❸ sexual activity

We were **fooling around** in the back of the car.

see also: MAKE OUT, NECK, PET, SMOOCH, SCREW AROUND

**fool around on** [fuːl əráund ɑn] v to commit ❸
adulterey

She was **fooling around on** her husband for years
before he found out.

   see also:  CHEAT, SLEEP AROUND, TWO-TIME

**fool with** [fuːl wiθ] v to disturb or play with ❶

Don't **fool with** the equipment, kids. It's very expensive
and delicate.

   see also:  MESS WITH

**"for Christsake!"** [fər kráis seik] inter [from for ❹
Christ's sake] expression of anger, frustration or
disappointment

**For Christsake**, stop playing the drums. It's after
midnight.

   see also:  CHRIST, DAMN, GOD, JESUS CHRIST

**"forget it"** [fərgét it] inter "You're mistaken" or "It's ❶
not important"

A: Why are you so angry at me? So, I forgot to return
   the movie. I'll take care of it.

B: **Forget it!** I'll return it to the video store myself.
   You're so unreliable!

   see also:  FAT CHANCE, NO WAY, YEAH RIGHT

**for keeps** [fər kíːps] adv forever ❶

You can have this **for keeps**. I won't be needing it back.

**for real** [fər ríːl] adj genuine, serious, sincere ❶

I don't think he's **for real**. He's says that he loves her,
but I don't think he really means it.

Are you **for real**?

   see also:  REAL

**for sure** [fər ʃúər, fər ʃɔ́ːr] *adv* certainly, definitely    ❶

I'm <u>gonna</u> see him tomorrow **for sure**, so do you want me to give him a message?

**For sure** he's the best frisbee player I've ever seen.

**foul** [faul] *adj* bad, lousy    ❶

That was some **foul** <u>shit</u> they fed us in the cafeteria. It tasted <u>gross</u>.

see also:  CRAPPY, CRUMMY, LAME, LOUSY, SHITTY

**foxy** [fɑksiː] *adj* sexy    ❸

Wow, check out the **foxy** <u>babe</u> standing on the corner.

see also:  HOT

**'fraid** [freid] *adj* [from *afraid*]    ❷

You **'fraid** of this little mouse?

**'fraidy cat** [fréidiː kæt] *n* a coward    ❷

Donny's too much of a **'fraidy cat** to jump in the pool.

see also:  CHICKEN, GUTLESS WONDER

**frame** [freim] *v* to create the appearance of guilt    ❶

Do you <u>really</u> believe that the cops tried to **frame** your father? I just don't <u>buy</u> that.

**frazzled** [fræzəld] *adj* exhausted    ❶

After a long day's work I usually feel pretty **frazzled**.

see also:  BEAT, BLEARY-EYED, BURNED OUT, BUSHED, DEAD, FRIED, OUT OF IT, POOPED, WASTED, WIPED OUT, ZONKED OUT

**freak** [friːk] *n* a weird person    ❸

That guy's a **freak**. How can you be in love with him?

see also:  BASKET CASE, FRUITCAKE, KOOK, NUTCASE, ODDBALL, SCREWBALL, WEIRDO, WHACKO

**freak (out)** [friːk áut] v to go crazy, to get angry  ❸

She **freaked** when she heard she was going to be fired.

When he took LSD for the first time he <u>really</u> **freaked out** and had to go the hospital.

He **freaked out** when he heard that his son had been arrested.

The girls **freaked out** when the band members walked on the stage.

see also:  BLOW A HAIRY, BLOW ONE'S COOL, FLIP, GO APESHIT, GO BANANAS, GO POSTAL, LOSE IT, LOSE ONE'S COOL

**freebie** [friːbiː] n something given without charge  ❶

I'm always glad to get **freebies** in the mail, but usually they're just junk.

see also:  FREE LUNCH

**freeloader** [friːloudər] n someone who imposes upon  ❶ the hospitality of others without sharing in the cost

Her boyfriend is a **freeloader**. He makes her work so he can stay home and watch TV.

**free lunch** [friː lʌntʃ] n something acquired without  ❶ effort or cost

Hey, there's no such thing as a **free lunch**.

see also:  FREEBIE

**fresh** [freʃ] adj rude, disrespectful  ❶

A:  Clean up your room Karen, it's a mess.

B:  Do it yourself Mom, I'm busy.

A:  Karen, don't get **fresh** with me, I said clean up your room!

see also:  SNOTTY, WISE

**frickin'/freakin'** [fríkin, frí:kiŋ] *int* [from *fucking*] ❹
added to express frustration, anger or surprise

That **frickin'** idiot told everybody my secret.

see also:  DAMNED, DOGGONED, FRIGGIN, FUCKING

**fried** [fraid] *adj* exhausted ❸

I felt <u>really</u> **fried** after that exam.

see also:  BEAT, BLEARY-EYED, BURNED OUT, BUSHED, DEAD,
FRAZZLED, OUT OF IT, POOPED, WASTED, WIPED OUT,
ZONKED OUT

**friggin'** [frígin] *int* [from *fucking*] added to express ❸
anger, annoyance

Get your **friggin'** car out of my driveway!

see also:  DAMNED, DOGGONED, FREAKIN, FRICKIN, FUCKING

**from the get-go** [frʌm ðə gét gou] *adv* from the ❶
beginning

He was lying to me **from the get-go**. I can't believe I
trusted him.

**from way back** [frʌm wéi bæk] *adv* for a long time ❶

We're friends **from way back**.

**front** [frʌnt] *n* mask, facade ❶

She smiles too much. Her happiness is just a **front**. I
know she's hiding something.

**fruitcake** [frú:tkeik] *n* a crazy person ❶

My neighbor's a <u>total</u> **fruitcake**. He talks to himself and
wears a purple woman's wig.

see also:  BASKET CASE, FREAK, KOOK, NUTCASE, ODDBALL,
SCREWBALL, WEIRDO, WHACKO

**frumpy** [frʌ́mpi:] *adj* old-fashioned, dowdy, ❶
unattractive

His mother is old and **frumpy**. She always looks like
she just got out of bed.

**fry** [frai] *v* to ruin, to destroy ❶

You're going to **fry** your speakers if you don't turn
down the volume.

He took too much LSD and **fried** his brain.

**fuck** [fʌk] *v* to have sex ❺

They were **fucking** in the back of the car.

see also:  BANG, FUCK, HUMP, MAKE LOVE, PORK, SCREW

**fuck** [fʌk] *n* act of sex ❺

I need a good **fuck**.

see also:  LAY, SCREW

**fuck** [fʌk] *n* a despicable person ❺

He's a real **fuck**. He would sell his own mother to make
a <u>buck</u>.

see also:  ASSHOLE, BASTARD, COCKSUCKER, CREEP, DICK,
DICKWEED, DIP, DIPSHIT, DOUCHE BAG, FUCKER, JERK,
MOTHERFUCKER, PRICK, SCHMUCK, SOB, SON OF A BITCH

**fuck (a)** [fʌk] *n* the least bit, a minimum degree ❺
(added for angry emphasis)

I don't give **a fuck** where you get it, I want the money
you owe me by tomorrow or you're a dead man.

see also:  DAMN

**"fuck!"** [fʌk] *inter* an expression of anger, frustration or ❺
surprise

**Fuck**! I burned myself on the stove.

see also:  DAMN, SHIT

**fucked** [fʌkt] *adj* in big trouble, dead, finished ❺

I'm **fucked**. When my boss finds out I've been stealing things from the office, he'll fire me for sure.

This car is **fucked**. Let's <u>ditch</u> it somewhere and go and find a new one.

see also:  DEAD, DONE FOR, SCREWED

**fucked up** [fʌkt ʌp] *adj* mentally sick, in a bad state, ❺

Anybody who would murder little children must <u>really</u> be **fucked up**.

She's been **fucked up** ever since she was raped.

The economic situation in the inner cities is <u>really</u> **fucked up**.

see also:  MESSED UP, SCREWED UP

**fucker** [fʌkər] *n* a bad person or thing ❺

Who's the **fucker** who ate all my chips?

see also:  ASSHOLE, BASTARD, COCKSUCKER, CREEP, DICK, DICKWEED, DIP, DIPSHIT, DOUCHE BAG, FUCK, JERK, MOTHERFUCKER, PRICK, SCHMUCK, SOB, SON OF A BITCH

**fucking** [fʌkin, fʌkiŋ] *int* added for emphasis ❺

I can't **fuckin'** believe you **fuckin'** lied to me you **fuckin'** <u>asshole</u>!

That **fucking** car can <u>really</u> <u>haul ass</u>!

see also:  DAMNED, DOGGONED, FREAKIN, FRICKIN, FRIGGIN

**"fuck it!"** [fʌk it] *inter* "My patience is exhausted!" ❺
"Forget it!"

**Fuck it**. Let's drive back to the hotel. In this traffic we'll never make it to the airport in time.

see also:  TO HELL WITH IT

**"fuck off!"** [fʌk ɔ́ːf] *imp* a pointed insult "Get out of     ❺
here!" "Leave!"

> **Fuck off!** I never want to see you again.

> Just tell him to **fuck off** if he starts <u>hitting on</u> you, <u>OK</u>?

> see also: BUG OFF, DROP DEAD, FUCK YOU, GET LOST, GO FUCK
> YOURSELF, GO TO HELL, SHOVE IT, SCREW YOU

**fuck (one) over** [fʌk wʌn óuvər] *v* to take     ❺
advantage of

> He has no friends left because he's **fucked them over**.

> A junkie would **fuck his mother over** for a fix.

> see also: SCREW

**fuck (over)** [fʌk óuvər] *v* to hurt or betray someone     ❺

> They say he changed his father's will, so when his
> father died, he inherited everything. He <u>really</u> **fucked
> over** his brothers and sisters.

> see also: DOUBLE-CROSS, SCREW, STAB IN THE BACK

**fuck that/this (shit)** [fʌk ðæt, ðis ʃit] *inter*     ❺
"Forget it!"

> He wants me to sleep with his friend <u>cuz</u> the guy is
> lonely? **Fuck that shit**. I ain't gonna sleep with nobody
> I don't love.

> see also: NO WAY

**fuck (the)** [ðə fʌk] *exp* added for angry emphasis     ❺

> Why **the fuck** are you late?

> What **the fuck** do you want?

> Who **the fuck** do you think you are?

> Where **the fuck** have you been! You were supposed to
> be here twenty minutes ago.

**fuck up** [fʌk ʌp] *v* to make a big mistake ❺

How could you curse at the boss? You <u>really</u> **fucked up** this time.

see also: MESS UP, SCREW UP

**fuckup** [fʌkʌp] *n* a big mistake, a failure ❺

I can't believe you told the President to shut up. That's a major **fuckup**.

I'm sorry I don't have your money. There was a big **fuckup** at the bank.

That guy's a <u>total</u> **fuckup**. He can't do anything right.

see also: LOSER

**fuck with** [fʌk wiθ] *v* to meddle with or threaten ❺

Hey, don't **fuck with** me <u>man</u> or I'll kill you.

see also: DICK AROUND, MESS WITH

**"fuck you!"** [fʌk júː] *imp* a very strong insult ❺
"Go to Hell!"

Hey, **fuck you**, <u>asshole</u>!

**fuddy-duddy** [fʌdiː dʌdiː] *n* a person who is ❷
old-fashioned or conservative

My dad is such a **fuddy-duddy**. He thinks bowling is the best thing in the world.

see also: KILLJOY, PARTY POOPER, STICK-IN-THE-MUD, WET BLANKET

**full of it/crap/mud** [ful əv it, kræp, mʌd] *adj* full ❹
of nonsense, deceitful

Those guys on the radio talking about the "New World Order" are **full of it**.

see also: FULL OF SHIT

**full of oneself** [ful əv wʌnself] *adj* conceited, ❹
self-absorbed

<u>God</u>, you are just so **full of yourself**. All you ever think
about is "me, me, me." Do you think that the world
revolves around you?

   see also: COCKY

**full of shit** [ful əv ʃit] *adj* deceitful, full of nonsense ❹

I can't believe how **full of shit** that <u>guy</u> is. He doesn't
love you, he just wants your money.

I think he's **full of shit**. He says he's slept with twenty
girls but I'll bet he hasn't slept with any.

   see also: FULL OF IT

**funk** [fʌŋk] *n* a state of depression ❸

She's been in a **funk** ever since her dog was run over by
a car.

   see also: BLAHS, BLUES, BUMMED, BUMMED OUT, DOWN

**funky** [fʌŋkiː] *adj* colorful and wild; having an odd or ❸
offensive odor

Her clothes are <u>really</u> **funky**. She's wearing jeans from
Mexico, a vest from Thailand, a hat from Jamaica and
earrings from Paris.

That band plays some <u>really</u> **funky** music.

Grace always wears these **funky** perfumes.

**fusspot** [fʌspɑt] *n* a person who complains constantly ❷

His aunt is a real **fusspot**. She complains about
everything.

**fussy** [fʌsiː] *adj* hard to please, whiny ❶

My cat's <u>really</u> **fussy**. She won't eat food from a box. She'll only eat real meat.

see also: PICKY

**fuzz** [fʌz] *n* the police ❹

The **fuzz** was <u>all over the place</u>.

see also: COP, PIG

# G

**gab** [gæb] *v* talk in a rapid or thoughtless manner ❶

There she is **gabbing** on the phone again.

see also: BLAB, YAK, YAP

**game** [geim] *adj* willing, ready to proceed ❶

Are you **game** for another hike tomorrow?

**garbage** [gárbidʒ] *n* nonsense, lies ❶

He's always talking **garbage** about how many problems he has.

see also: BALONEY, BULLSHIT, CRAP, JIVE, RUBBISH, TRASH

**gas** [gæs] *n* fun, a good time ❶

We had a <u>real</u> **gas** at your party last night.

see also: BLAST, PISSER, RIOT

**gas guzzler** [gǽs gʌzlər] *n* a car with poor fuel efficiency ❶

This old car only gets 5 miles to the gallon. It's a <u>real</u> **gas guzzler**.

**geek** [giːk] *n* an overly studious or socially awkward ❸
person

He's a big **geek**. All he ever does is study.

  see also:  DORK, DRIP, DWEEB, NERD

**"gee (whiz)!"** [dʒiː wiz] *inter* expression of ❷
enthusiasm, surprise, or dismay

**Gee**, I'm <u>really</u> glad to see you.

**Gee**, that sunset's beautiful.

**Gee** George, you look great today!

**Gee whiz**, I'm sorry I hit your car.

**Gee**, I thought I brought the key with me, but I must
have left it at home.

  see also:  DAG, DANG, DARN, DRAT, GOLLY, GOOD GRIEF, GOSH,
       JEEZ, RATS, SHOOT

**geezer** [giːzər] *n* an odd or eccentric old man ❸

  A: Who's that old **geezer** standing by your door?

  B: That's my grandfather. Show some respect!

  see also:  OLD FART

**"get a brain!"** [get ə bréin] *imp* "Get serious!" ❸
"Don't be so stupid!"

You think the earth is flat? **Get a brain!**

  see also:  GET A CLUE

**"get a clue!"** [get ə klúː] *imp* "Face the facts!" ❸
"Become informed!"

She doesn't return your calls? Well, **get a clue** <u>man</u>.
Maybe she doesn't want to talk to you.

  see also:  GET A BRAIN

**get a handle on** [get ə hǽndl ɑn] *v* to understand, ❶
to control

I think I am beginning to **get a handle on** what you are
trying to say.

You need to **get a handle on** your emotions so that you
can accept criticism.

**"get a life!"** [get ə láif] *imp* "Lead a realistic life!" ❸

I can't believe you spend so much time watching porno
films. **Get a life!**

**"get a load of..."** [get ə lóud əv] *inter* "Look ❸
at that!"

**Get a load of** the hair on that girl! It's green and
yellow.

see also: CHECK IT OUT

**"get a move on!"** [get ə múːv ɑn] *imp* "Move ❶
quickly!"

Don't stand around with your hands in your pockets.
**Get a move on!**

**get anywhere** [get éniːwɛər] *v* to make progress ❶

I've been studying Spanish for years, but I can't seem to
**get anywhere** with it.

**get back at** [get bǽk æt] *v* to take revenge ❶

My son tries to **get back at** me by refusing to eat his
dinner.

**get by** [get bái] *v* manage ❶

We're not rich, but we **get by**.

see also: COPE, MAKE OUT

**get his/get hers** [get hiz, get hərz] v to get one's ❶
due, to get what one has coming

He'll **get his** someday. Just wait and see.

**get hitched** [get hitʃt] v to get married ❶

They **got hitched** last year in Hawaii.

**get hosed** [get houzd] v to get treated badly, to be ❶
beaten decisively in sports

I **got hosed** by the plumber. He charged me five
hundred dollars just to replace one piece of pipe.

see also: GET SCREWED, GET SHAFTED

**get into** [get íntu:] v to become involved ❶

She only started studying English last year, but she's
really **getting into** it. She studies three hours a day and
has improved a lot.

I just can't **get into** my new job. I think I'm gonna bag
it soon.

see also: INTO

**get it** [get it] v to understand ❶

I don't **get it**. She says she loves me but she doesn't
want to marry me.

That's the funniest joke I ever heard. Hey Bob, why
aren't you laughing? Don't you **get it**?

see also: CATCH ON, FIGURE OUT

**get it up** [get it ʌp] v to have an erection ❺

My boyfriend couldn't **get it up** last night. Boy, was he
embarrassed.

93

**"get lost!"** [get lɔːst] *imp* "Get out of here!"  ❹

**Get lost!** I never want to see you again.

see also: BUG OFF, DROP DEAD

**"get off my case!"** [get ɔːf mai kéis] *imp* "Stop  ❸
badgering me!"

A: Harry, have you done your homework today?

B: <u>C'mon</u> <u>Mom</u>, **get off my case** <u>already</u> will <u>ya</u>? Can't
you see I'm in the middle of doing it?

see also: GET OUT OF MY FACE

**get off on** [get ɔːf ɑn] *v* to derive pleasure from  ❹

He **gets off on** hurting little animals. The <u>guy</u> is sick.

see also: GET ONE'S ROCKS OFF

**get off someone's case** [get ɔːf sʌmwʌnz kéis]  ❹
*v* to leave one alone, stop badgering

Why don't you **get off his case**. He's had enough
criticism for one day.

**get one's act together** [get wʌnz ǽkt tuːgeðər]  ❶
*v* to organize one's life

If you don't **get your act together**, I'm leaving you.

We need to **get our act together** if we want our
relationship to survive.

see also: GET ONE'S SHIT TOGETHER, HAVE ONE'S SHIT
TOGETHER

**get one's rocks off** [get wʌnz rɑks ɔːf] *v* to  ❹
sexually or perversely enjoy

That <u>guy's</u> a pervert. He **gets his rocks off** by fondling
girls on the train.

see also: GET OFF ON

94

### get one's shit together [get wʌnz ʃít tu:geðər] ❹
v to improve one's habits or organize one's affairs

If you don't **get your shit together**, I'm <u>gonna</u> kick you out of this house.

That girl <u>really</u> has **got her shit together**.

see also: GET ONE'S ACT TOGETHER, HAVE ONE'S SHIT TOGETHER

### "get out of here!"/"get outta here!" [get áut əv hier, gedáudəhiər] inter "You're kidding!" ❸

**Get outta here**! I can't believe it. How did you know it was <u>really</u> him?

see also: NO SHIT, YEAH RIGHT

### "get out of my face!" [get áut əv mai feis] imp ❹
"Leave me alone!" "Stop badgering me!"

Why are you screaming at me? **Get out of my face** <u>already</u>!

see also: GET OFF MY CASE

### get over [get óuvər] v to overcome, recover ❶

I'm **getting over** a cold.

She can't **get over** him. Even though he left her last year she still loves him.

### get psyched [get sáikt] v to become excited and energized ❸

Come on guys, **get psyched**! We <u>gotta</u> win this game.

If <u>ya</u> <u>wanna</u> win ya <u>gotta</u> **get psyched**.

### "get real!" [get ri:l] imp "Be realistic!" ❸

**Get real**, <u>man</u>. You can't afford a yacht.

see also: GET SERIOUS

## get screwed [get skruːd] v to be cheated ❹

She **got screwed** by her insurance company. They refused to pay for the earthquake damage to her house.

see also: GET HOSED, GET SHAFTED

## "get serious!" [get siːrjəs] *imp* "Be realistic!" ❶

**Get serious!** You can't go into politics with your criminal record.

see also: GET REAL

## get the ax [get ðiː æks] v to get fired ❶

Twenty thousand steel workers **got the ax** last year.

see also: LAY OFF, SACK

## "get the fuck outta here!" [get ðə fʌk áutə hiər] ❺

*inter* "You're kidding!"

What? You're pregnant? **Get the fuck outta here!**

see also: NO SHIT, NO WAY, BULLSHIT

## get the shaft/get shafted [get ðə ʃæft, get ʃæftəd] ❸

v to be treated badly, to be cheated

Don't go to work for Leon or you're liable to **get shafted**.

Don <u>really</u> **got the shaft** when he divorced his wife. She got the house, the car, and his record collection.

see also: GET HOSED, GET SCREWED

## get together [get tuːgéðər] v to meet or gather ❶

Are you busy tonight? I was thinking we could **get together** and see a movie.

The whole family **got together** for a big Christmas meal.

see also: HANG OUT

**get up and go** [get ʌp ən góu] *n* energy ❶

I don't like people who have no **get up and go**.

see also: PEP, PIZZAZZ, SPARK, SPUNK

**"get with it!"** [get wíθ it] *imp* "Become aware!" "Be ❶
current!"

You still wear polyester pants? **Get with it!** They went
out of style years ago.

**get with it** [get wíθ it] *v* to become aware, to be ❶
current

If you want a job in the computer industry, you'd better
**get with it**. You need to graduate from an accredited
university.

**ghetto blaster** [gedou blǽstər] *n* somewhat ❸
derogatory term for a large portable radio or tape player

Turn that <u>damned</u> **ghetto blaster** down! I can't hear
myself think!

see also: BOOM BOX

**"gimme a break!"** [gimi:jə bréik] *inter* "Be serious!" ❶
"You must be joking!"

What do you mean you bought a fur coat? **Gimme a
break!** You know we can't afford such luxury. I want
you to return it to the store right away!

see also: COME OFF IT, CUT ONE SOME SLACK

**gimmick** [gímik] *n* a trick or deception ❶

A: They're offering a five hundred dollar rebate if you
buy their car.

B: It's just a **gimmick**. They raised the sticker price by
five hundred dollars.

**girl** [gərl] *n* a woman (some women find this sexist) ❸

Hey **girl**, do you love me?

Whoa! <u>Check out</u> those **girls** over there.

see also:  BABE, BROAD, CHICK

**girlie magazine** [gɚli: mægəzí:n] *n* a magazine ❶
featuring pictures of scantily clad women

He reads **girlie magazines** after his wife leaves for
work.

**"give it to me straight!"** [giv it tu: mi: stréit] *imp* ❶
"Tell the truth!" "Be frank!"

**Give it to me straight** <u>baby</u>, are you <u>sleeping around</u>
on me?

see also:  LAY IT ON SOMEONE, TELL IT LIKE IT IS

**give one a break** [giv wʌn ə breik] *v* to give a ❶
chance or special consideration

Why don't you **give the kid a break** and let him keep
his job. I don't think he'll be late again.

**give one head** [giv wʌn hed] *v* perform cunnilingus ❺
or fellatio

If a man can't **give me** good **head** I don't enjoy sex.

She **gave Bill head**.

see also:  BLOWJOB, GO DOWN ON

**give someone the cold shoulder** [giv sʌmwʌn
ðə kould ʃóuldɚ] *v* to treat badly, ignore ❶

I felt <u>really</u> tense at the party because the host was
**giving me the cold shoulder**.

see also:  COLD SHOULDER, SILENT TREATMENT

**gizmo** [gízmou] *n* a gadget ❶

What's this **gizmo** for? It looks like a little robot.

see also:  DOOHICKEY, THINGAMAJIG, WHATCHAMACALLIT

**glitzy** [glítsiː] *adj* extravagant, ostentatious ❶

Parisian fashion is often too **glitzy** for me.

see also: POSH, RITZY, SNAZZY

**glob** [glɑb] *n* a small clump of material ❶

There was a **glob** of <u>snot</u> on his nose.

**glom** [glɑm] *v* to adhere to ❸

David **glommed** on to Eric when he realized he could use him for free publicity.

**gnarly** [nárliː] *adj* dirty, rough, exciting, excellent ❸

His underwear was <u>really</u> **gnarly** because he hadn't changed for a week.

We had a <u>really</u> **gnarly** time climbing down the mountain. I though we were <u>gonna</u> die.

The waves at North Shore were <u>really</u> **gnarly**!

see also: GONZO, RAD

**go apeshit** [gou eipʃit] *v* to become very angry or ❹ crazy

When he heard about his girlfriend cheating on him he **went apeshit** and nearly hit her.

see also: BLOW A HAIRY, BLOW ONE'S COOL, FLIP, FREAK, GO BANANAS, GO POSTAL, LOSE IT, LOSE ONE'S COOL

**go bananas** [gou bənǽnəs] *v* to become very angry ❶ or crazy

He **went bananas** after his wife ruined the pot roast.

see also: BLOW A HAIRY, BLOW ONE'S COOL, FLIP, FREAK, GO APESHIT, GO POSTAL, LOSE IT, LOSE ONE'S COOL

**gobbledygook** [gabəldi:guk] *n* confusing jargon, ❶
nonsense; something unintelligible

Legal language is **gobbledygook** to me.

see also: BULLSHIT, LEGALESE

**go bonkers** [gou bánkərz] *v* to go insane ❶

He **went bonkers** after taking too many drugs.

see also: LOSE IT, LOSE ONE'S MARBLES

**"God!"** [gɑd] *inter* expression of anger, frustration, ❶
amazement

**God**, I can't believe you're forty years old. You look at
most twenty-five.

**God**! She makes me so angry! I can't stand her <u>attitude</u>.

see also: CHRIST, DAMN, FOR CHRISTSAKE, JESUS CHRIST

**godforsaken** [gàdfərséikən] *adj* remote, desolate ❶

Let's get out of this **godforsaken** place.

**go down** [gou dáun] *v* to occur, to take place ❸

The <u>cops</u> are waiting for the drug bust to **go down**.

**go down on** [gou dáun ɑn] *v* perform fellatio or ❺
cunnilingus

She **went down on** him on their first date.

see also: BLOWJOB, GIVE ONE HEAD

**go down the tubes** [gou daun ðə tú:bz] *v* to fail ❶
utterly

His idea of being his own boss **went down the tubes**
after his business failed.

see also: CRASH AND BURN

**go Dutch** [gou dʌtʃ] v to share expenses ❶

He's so <u>cheap</u>, he always **goes Dutch**, even with his girlfriend.

**go for it** [góufərit] v to use all of one's effort ❶

A: I was thinking of writing a book about my experiences during the war.

B: You should **go for it**! When are you going to start?

see also: GO TO THE MAX

**"go fuck yourself!"** [gou fʌk yərself] imp a very ❻ coarse insult: "Go to hell!"

A: <u>Drop dead</u> <u>asshole</u>!

B: Oh, **go fuck yourself**!

see also: BUG OFF, DROP DEAD, FUCK OFF, FUCK YOU, GET LOST, GO TO HELL, SHOVE IT, SCREW YOU

**go-getter** [gougétər] n an ambitious person ❶

That kid's selling lemonade to the neighbors. He's a <u>real</u> **go-getter**.

**"golly!"** [gɔ́ːliː, gɑliː] int expression of surprise, ❷ frustration

**Golly**, I didn't know you could drive.

see also: DAG, DANG, GEE, GOOD GRIEF, GOSH, JEEZ, SHOOT

**gonna'** [gʌ́nə] contr [from going to] ❶

I'm **gonna'** go to America next year.

**go nuts** [gou nʌtz] v to be crazy, enthusiastic ❶

Oedipus **went nuts** when he realized he had slept with his mother.

This place is going to **go nuts** when you come through the door.

see also: GO BONKERS, GO BANANAS

**gonzo** [gánzou] *adj* wild, out of control ❸

When it comes to surfing, that dude's got a <u>real</u> **gonzo** <u>attitude</u>.

He went **gonzo** when he heard that another scriptwriter had stolen his idea.

see also: GNARLY, RAD

**good egg** [gud ég] *n* a nice person ❷

That kid's a **good egg**.

see also: GOOD KID

**good for nothin** [gúd fər nʌθin] *adj* bad, useless ❹

He's a **good for nothin'** <u>son of a bitch</u>.

**good goin'** [gud góuin] *inter* [from *good going*] ❶
"Congratulations!"

You won the race? **Good goin'**!

**"good grief!"** [gud grí:f] *inter* expression of surprise ❶
or frustration

**Good grief**! Look at how many cars were in that accident!

see also: DAG, DANG, GEE, GOLLY, GOSH, JEEZ

**good kid** [gud kíd] *n* a loyal or reliable person, ❷
usually young

He's a **good kid**. You can trust him.

see also: GOOD EGG

**good-looking/best-looking** [gud lúkiŋ] ❶
*adj* handsome or pretty

Wow, who's that **good-looking** <u>guy</u> over there?

He's the **best-looking** boy in the school.

see also: CUTE, GORGEOUS

### "goodness gracious!" [gudnes gréiʃis] ❶
int expression of pleasant surprise

**Goodness gracious**, you're five years old? You're a big boy aren't you!

see also: GOOD GRIEF

### good shit [gud ʃít] n a high-quality item ❹

I always buy my <u>coke</u> from them. They've got some <u>real</u> **good shit**.

### "goody!" [gúdiː] inter "Great!" ❷

**Goody**! Now we're going to get ice cream!

### goody-goody two shoes [gùdiː gùdiː túː ʃuːz] ❷
n a child who curries favor

She's a **goody-goody two shoes**. The teachers love her but the kids hate her.

see also: ASS KISSER, BROWNNOSER,

### goof/goofball [guːf, gúːfbɔːl] n a silly or clumsy ❶
person

Jim's a <u>real</u> **goof**. He can't do anything right.

see also: AIRHEAD, BIRDBRAIN, BLOCKHEAD, BONEHEAD, BOZO, CRETIN, DIMWIT, DINGBAT, DITZ, DODO, DOPE, DUMBELL, DUMMY, KNUCKLEHEAD, LAMEBRAIN, MEATHEAD, NINCOMPOOP, NUMBSKULL, PEA-BRAIN, RETARD, SCATTERBRAIN, SPACE CADET, TWIT

### goof off [guːf ɔːf] v to shirk work or responsibility ❶

Are you reading comic books again? If you keep **goofing off** during working hours the boss is going to fire you.

see also: FART AROUND

**goofy** [gúːfiː] *adj* silly ❶

Why are you acting so **goofy**? Are you drunk?

see also: KLUTZY, SPASTIC

**go on and on** [gou ɑn ən ɑ́n] *v* to talk incessantly, ❶
to complain

She was **going on and on** about how she loves her cat.
It was <u>really</u> boring.

He **went on and on** for at least an hour about how he
hates his job.

see also: BITCH, CARRY ON, GRIPE, SOUND OFF

**go out** [gou áut] *v* to see someone socially, to date ❶
someone

They've been **going out** for seven years. But I think
they're about to <u>break up</u> because she doesn't love him
anymore.

**go postal** [gou póustəl] *v* to go berserk, to become ❸
violently crazy

He has a scary <u>edge</u> about him. He looks like he might
**go postal** any second.

see also: BLOW A HAIRY, BLOW ONE'S COOL, FLIP, FREAK, GO
APESHIT, GO BANANAS, LOSE IT, LOSE ONE'S COOL

**gorgeous** [gɔ́ːrdʒis] *adj* handsome ❸

You are so **gorgeous** I can't stand it!

see also: CUTE, GOOD-LOOKING

**"gosh!"** [gɑʃ] *inter* to express surprise, frustration, or ❷
disappoinment

**Gosh**, I didn't know you could play the guitar so well.

**Gosh** Mr. Jones, I didn't know you knew how to
rollerblade.

see also: DAG, DANG, GEE, GOLLY, GOOD GRIEF, JEEZ, SHOOT

**go steady** [gou stédi:] v to date one person exclusively ❸

I hear that Eric and Jane are **going steady**.

see also: GO OUT

**"gotcha!"** [gátʃə] *inter* [from *I've got you*] ❶

**Gotcha**! You kids can't hide from me!

see also: SNAG

**go the whole nine yards** [gou ðə houl nain járdz] v to do all that is necessary ❸

I want a perfect wedding ceremony. Let's **go the whole nine yards**.

**got it made** [gat it méid] *adj* successful, prosperous ❶

Man, you've **got it made**. You're rich and you have a beautiful wife.

**"go to hell!"** [gou tu: hél] *imp* a pointed insult "Get out of here!" ❹

**Go to hell!** I never want to see you again!

see also: BUG OFF, DROP DEAD, FUCK OFF, FUCK YOU, GET LOST, GO FUCK YOURSELF, GO TO HELL, SHOVE IT, SCREW YOU

**go to the max** [gou tu: ðə mæx] v to expend great effort ❸

I want you to **go to the max** for me and win a gold medal.

see also: GO FOR IT

**gotta** [gádə] *contr* [from *got to*] ❶

I **gotta** go home now. It's already ten PM.

**gramma** [grǽma] *n* [from *grandmother*] ❷

My **gramma's** eighty.

**grampa** [grǽmpɑ] *n* [from *grandfather*]  ❷

My **grampa** married my <u>gramma</u> fifty years ago.

**grass** [græs] *n* marijuana  ❸

**Grass** is illegal, but I think it's a milder drug than alcohol.

see also:  DOPE, HASH, POT, WEED

**"great"** [greit] *inter* expression of excitement or  ❶
happiness; disappointment or frustration

**Great**! I got an "A" on my math test!

Oh **great**. I've got a flat tire.

see also:  AWESOME, DYNAMITE, EXCELLENT, FAR OUT, OUT OF
SIGHT, RIGHT ON, WOW

**greatest (the)** [ðə grɛ́itəst] *n* the best, a great thing  ❶
or person

Dad, you're **the greatest**.

**grind** [graind] *n* a boring or tedious situation  ❶

Man, my job is such a **grind**.

see also:  BUMMER, DOWNER, DRAG, PITS

**gripe** [graip] *n* a complaint  ❶

He has a lot of **gripes** about his boss.

**gripe** [graip] *v* to complain  ❶

He keeps **griping** about his job.

see also:  BITCH, CARRY ON, GO ON AND ON, SOUND OFF

**grody** [groudiː] *adj* disgusting, dirty  ❸

His pants are <u>really</u> **grody**. I wish he'd wash them once
in a while!

see also:  CRUDDY, DINGY, GNARLY, GROSS, ICKY, YUCKY

**gross** [grous] *adj* disgusting ❸

His face is covered with pimples and warts. It's <u>really</u> **gross**. I feel sorry for him.

see also: GNARLY, GROSS, ICKY, YUCKY

**"gross!"** [grous] *inter* "Disgusting!" ❸

**Gross**! There's a dead mouse in the closet!

**gross someone out** [grous sʌmwʌn aut] ❸
*v* to disgust someone

I think you act that way just to **gross me out**.

see also: TURN OFF

**grouch** [grautʃ] *n* an irritable or cranky person ❶

I can't stand being around him. He's such a **grouch**.

see also: CRANK, SOURPUSS

**grouchy** [gráutʃiː] *adj* irritable, cranky ❶

<u>Dad</u> is always **grouchy** when he's having trouble at work.

see also: CRABBY

**grub** [grʌb] *n* food ❶

Hey <u>man</u>, I'm starving. Got any **grub**?

see also: CHOW, MUNCHIES

**grungy** [grʌndʒiː] *adj* dirty, sloppy in appearance ❸

Sometimes teenagers think it's <u>cool</u> to look **grungy**.

see also: DINGY, GNARLY

**guess** [ges] *v* to think, to suppose ❶

It's already eleven. I **guess** I'll go to bed soon.

see also: FIGURE

**"guess what!"** [ges wʌ́t] *inter* "Listen to this!"  ❶

Guess what! We're getting married!

Guess what! I saw the mayor in the supermarket today!

**gung ho** [gʌŋ hóu] *adj* excited, enthusiastic  ❶

Only naive people are **gung ho** about war.

see also: KEEN, PSYCHED, PUMPED

**gunk** [gʌŋk] *n* dirt  ❶

What's this **gunk** on my shoes? It looks like glue.

see also: CRUD

**gun one's engine** [gʌn wʌnz éndʒin] *v* to make a  ❶
loud sound with the engine of one's car.

He kept **gunning his engine** to show how mad he was.

**gut** [gʌt] *n* a big belly  ❶

Who's the slob over there with his **gut** hanging out?

see also: BEER BELLY

**gutless** [gʌ́tlis] *adj* cowardly, spineless  ❶

He's the most **gutless** guy I've ever met.

see also: CHICKEN

**gutless wonder** [gʌtlis wʌ́ndər] *n* coward  ❸

Dave's a **gutless wonder**. He's even afraid of riding a bike.

see also: CHICKEN, 'FRAIDY-CAT

**guts** [gʌts] *n* courage ❸

I think skydiving takes a lot of **guts**. Either that or you have to be pretty crazy.

see also:  BALLS, CHUTZPAH

**gutsy** [gʌtziː] *adj* courageous, brave ❶

She's <u>really</u> **gutsy**. She's not afraid of anybody or anything.

see also:  BALLSY

**guy** [gai] *n* a boy or man, a person or persons ❶

Who's that handsome **guy** she's with?

Hi you **guys**, how <u>ya</u> doin'?

see also:  BUD, DUDE, MAN

# H

**had (to be)** [tuː biː hæd] *v* to be tricked or deceived ❶

I've **been had**. I thought I was buying real gold, but it's <u>phony</u>.

see also:  CON, SHORTCHANGE

**hairy** [héəriː] *adj* scary, threatening ❸

We thought the typhoon was going to blow our house down. It was a <u>real</u> **hairy** situation.

**half-assed** [hæfǽst] *adj* careless, incomplete ❹

If you're gonna' do a **half-assed** job, don't do it at all.

We lost the game because of our **half-assed** playing.

**ham** [hæm] *n* a comedian, an overacting performer ❶

He's such a **ham**. He's always trying to make everybody laugh.

see also: JOKER

**hammered** [hǽmərd] *adj* drunk ❶

We stayed out all night and got <u>really</u> **hammered**.

see also: PLASTERED, SHITFACED, SLOSHED, SMASHED, WASTED

**hang** [hæŋ] *v* to loiter, linger ❶

Let's go **hang** in front of the mall.

see also: CHILL, FART AROUND, GOOF OFF, HANG OUT

**hang a left/right** [hæŋ ə left, rait] *v* to turn ❶
left/right

**Hang a left** at the light.

I **hung a right** and then **hung a left**.

**hang around** [hæŋ əráund] *v* to loiter ❶

I called the <u>cops</u> <u>cuz</u> this weird-looking <u>guy</u> was **hanging around** outside my apartment.

**hang in there** [hæŋ ín ðɛer] *v* to persist, persevere ❶

A: How's Donny? I heard he has cancer.

B: He's **hanging in there**, but we're all worried.

**Hang in there** Tom. They'll send a helicopter to rescue you soon.

see also: STICK IT OUT

**hang out** [hæŋ áut] *v* to loiter or linger ❶

I like **hanging out** with my friends at the pizza parlor.

see also: CHILL, FART AROUND, GOOF OFF, HANG

**hangout** [hǽŋaut] *n* a place where people gather ❶

The criminals went to their **hangout** after the robbery.

see also: JOINT

**hang-up** [hǽŋʌp] *n* a source of mental difficulty ❶

She won't have sex with me unless I take a shower first. She has a real **hang-up** about cleanliness.

see also: THING

**hanky** [hǽŋkiː] *n* [from *handkerchief*] ❶

Could you pass me a **hanky** please? I have to blow my nose.

**hanky-panky** [hǽŋkiː pǽŋkiː] *n* questionable ❷
activity, sexual activity

There was some **hanky-panky** going on in the back of their car.

see also: NOOKY

**hard-ass** [hárdæs] *n* a tough, mean person ❹

My teacher is such a **hard-ass**. He makes us learn a new Latin poem every day.

see also: BALL BUSTER

**hard-assed** [hárdæst] *adj* tough, mean ❹

He's got a real **hard-assed** attitude.

**hardly** [hárdliː] *adv* to a minimal degree ❶

I can't ask him that! I **hardly** know him.

**hard-on** [hárdɔːn] *n* an erection ❺

Whenever he sees pictures of naked women he gets a **hard-on**.

see also: BONER, WOODY

**hard up** [hɑrd ʌp] *adj* desperate, in need of ❸

Can you help out my friend? He's <u>really</u> **hard up** for work.

Jack hasn't slept with a woman in a year. He's pretty **hard up**.

**harebrained** [héər breind] *adj* foolish, outlandish ❶

That is the most **harebrained** idea I've ever heard.

    see also:  COCKAMAMIE

**has-been** [hǽz bin] *n* someone or something past its ❶
prime

Some people were saying he was already a **has-been** before his new album came out.

**hash** [hæʃ] *n* [from *hashish*] an extract of the ❶
marijauna plant smoked for its intoxicating qualities

We usually smoke <u>grass</u> because it's so hard to find **hash** around here.

    see also:  DOPE, GRASS, POT, WEED

**hassle** [hæsl] *n* problem, difficulty ❶

<u>Man</u>, I hate this job. It's one **hassle** after another

**hassle** [hæsl] *v* to annoy ❶

Look, don't **hassle** me about the kids, <u>OK</u>? I had a hard day at work and the last thing I need is to come home and get **hassled** by my wife.

    see also:  BUG, PESTER

**hasta la vista** [ɑstɑ lə víːstɑ] *inter* "Goodbye" ❸
[from Spanish for *Until the horizon*]

**Hasta la vista** <u>guys</u>. I <u>gotta</u> go.

**haul ass** [hɔːl æs] *v* to hurry, to move quickly  ❹

Hey <u>man</u>, if you <u>wanna</u> make the train, you're <u>gonna</u> have to **haul ass**.

see also: BOOGIE, BOOK, CLEAR OUT, HIGHTAIL IT, HUSTLE, SPLIT, STEP ON IT, VAMOOSE

**have a ball** [hæv ə bɔːl] *v* to have fun, enjoy  ❶

That was a great party. Thanks for inviting me. I **had a ball**.

see also: PARTY

**have one's head examined** [hæv wʌnz hέd egzǽmind] *exp* said of one who is regarded as crazy or wrong  ❶

He's wrecked every car he's ever driven and you lent your car to him? I think you need to **have your head examined**.

**have one's act/shit together** [hæv wʌnz ǽkt, ʃít tuːgέðər] *v* to be organized, successful  ❶ ❹

<u>Give him a break</u>! He's trying to **get his act together**.

She <u>really</u> **has her shit together**.

**headache** [hέdeik] *n* annoyance  ❶

My kid is a real **headache**. All he does is cry, cry, cry.

see also: PAIN, PAIN IN THE NECK, TROUBLE

**head honcho** [hed hántʃou] *n* the boss or chief  ❸

Who's the **head honcho** around here?

see also: BIG SHOT, HEAVY, VIP

**head off** [hed ɔːf] *v* to depart, begin a journey  ❶

He's **heading off** to Mexico tomorrow.

**head out** [hed áut] *v* to leave ❶

It's time to **head out**. It's getting late.

**heap** [hi:p] *n* an automobile that is in poor condition ❶

My car's a **heap**, but at least it runs.

see also: CLUNKER, JALOPY

**heart** [hɑrt] *n* courage, determination ❶

That boy has a lot of **heart**. He never gives up.

see also: SOUL

**heave** [hi:v] *v* to vomit ❸

That sushi didn't agree with me. I think I'm going to **heave**.

see also: BARF, BOOT, PUKE, THROW UP

**heavy** [hévi:] *n* an influential or powerful person, VIP ❶

He's a real **heavy** in the world of literature.

see also: BIG SHOT, HEAD HONCHO, VIP

**heavy** [hévi:] *adj* serious, oppressive ❶

Why do you have to be so **heavy** all the time? Why don't you lighten up a bit?

**heavy shit** [hévi: ʃit] *n* serious or intense issues ❹

That was some _real_ **heavy shit** he was talkin' about in there.

**heinie** [háini:] *n* buttocks ❷

Get your **heinie** over here and get busy!

see also: ASS, BOTTOM, BUM, BUNS, BUTT, FANNY, REAR END

**hell (the)** [ðe hel] *exp* added to express anger, surprise, frustration ❹

Why **the hell** did you tell her I had been in prison?

**helluva** [hélʌvə] *adj* [from *hell of a*] very, exceedingly ❹

He's a **helluva** nice guy.

That was a **helluva** stupid thing to say.

**here and there** [hiərənðɛər] *adv* many places, no specific place ❶

A: Today we walked around New York.

B: Where'd ya go?

A: Oh, we just went **here and there**.

see also: ALL OVER, EVERY WHICH WAY

**hick** [hik] *n* insulting term for a rural or uneducated person ❹

He grew up in New York City but married some **hick** from the Midwest.

see also: COUNTRY BUMPKIN

**hickey** [híki:] *n* a temporary skin blotch from a passionate kiss ❸

She was embarrassed because she had a **hickey** on her neck.

**high** [hai] *adj* under the influence of a drug; lively or excited ❸

Everybody smoked hash and got really **high**.

Ever since he became head-manager he's been feeling really **high**.

see also: PUMPED, PSYCHED, STONED, WASTED

**highfalutin'** [háifəluːtin] *adj* pretentious, arrogant ❶

What a snob. She has a <u>real</u> **highfalutin'** <u>attitude</u>.

see also: ATTITUDE, COCKY, SNOOTY, SNOTTY, STUCK UP, UPPITY

**high-strung** [hai strʌ́ŋ] *adj* having a nervous ❶
personality

I don't like **high-strung** <u>guys</u>. I prefer the <u>laid-back</u> type.

see also: ANTSY, UPTIGHT

**hightail it** [háiteil it] *v* to depart quickly ❶

We **hightailed it** out of there when the <u>cops</u> showed up.

see also: BOOGIE, BOOK, CLEAR OUT, HAUL ASS, HUSTLE, SPLIT, STEP ON IT, VAMOOSE

**hip** [hip] *adj* in fashion ❶

The decor in this restaurant is <u>really</u> **hip**. I wonder who designed it?

see also: BAD, COOL, NEAT, SLICK

**hippie** [hípiː] *n* a person who acts like a 1960's rebel, ❶
with unconventional, often anti-establishment attitudes

My brother is a **hippie**. He lives at a farm co-op, smokes <u>pot</u>, and plays the guitar all day.

**history** [hístəriː] *adj* finished ❸

If I fail this test I'm **history**. I'll have to take the course over again.

Communism is **history**. Soon, all nations will be democracies.

see also: DEAD, DONE FOR

**hit on** [hít ɔːn] *v* to make sexual advances ❶

I beat him up <u>cuz</u> he was **hitting on** my girlfriend.

see also: COME ON TO

**hit the hay** [hit ðə héi] *v* to go to bed, to sleep ❶

<u>OK</u> kids, it's time to **hit the hay**.

see also: CATCH SOME Z'S, CONK OUT, SNOOZE

**hit the jackpot** [hit ðə dʒǽkpɑt] *v* to be highly ❶
successful, to strike it rich

He <u>really</u> **hit the jackpot** when he married her. She's
rich, smart, and beautiful. I just don't understand why
she would marry a <u>loser</u> like him.

**hog** [hɑg] *n* a greedy person ❶

Hey, leave some pie for the rest of us! Don't be such a
**hog**.

see also: PIG

**hog** [hɑg] *v* to take more than one's fair share ❶

Stop **hogging** the TV. You've been watching football for
six hours.

**"hold on!"** [hould án] *imp* "Wait!" ❶

**Hold on** please, I'll get to you just as soon as I can.

**Hold on** just one minute. You can't talk to me like that!

see also: HOLD YOUR HORSES, JUST A SEC

**holdup** [hóuld ʌp] *n* robbery ❶

There was a **holdup** at the bank the other day.

see also: STICKUP

117

**hold up** [hóuld ʌp] *v* to rob ❶

The first thing he did when he got out of prison was to **hold up** a bank.

see also: STICK UP

**"hold your horses"** [hould jər hɔ́rsəz] *imp* "Slow ❶ down!" "Be patient!"

**Hold your horses!** I didn't say I was going to buy you a car. I said I would think about it.

see also: JUST A SEC, HOLD ON

**hole up** [houl ʌp] *v* to hide ❶

Let's go to Utah and **hole up** in a motel until the FBI stops looking for us.

**"Holy Moly!"** [houli: móuli:] *inter* [from *Holy Moses*] ❶ expression of anger, frustration or surprise

**Holy Moly**, that's the biggest rat I've ever seen.

see also: HOLY SMOKES, OH MY GOD

**"holy shit!"** [houli: ʃít] *inter* expression of anger, ❹ frustration or surprise

**Holy shit!** The house is on fire! Call the fire department!

see also: CHRIST, DAMN, GOD, JESUS CHRIST

**"holy smokes!"** [houli: smóuks] *inter* expression of ❶ anger, frustration or surprise

**Holy smokes!** There's the President!

see also: HOLY MOLY, OH MY GOD

**homeboy/homie** [hóumbɔi, hóumi:] *n* term for ❸ people from one's neighborhood, friends

I'm going to party with some of my **homies**.

**honey** [hʌ́niː] *exp* term of endearment ❶

**Honey**, have you seen my keys?

see also: BABY, LOVEY, SWEETIE

**honey** [hʌ́niː] *n* one's lover, wife, husband, boyfriend, ❶
girlfriend, etc

He's taking his **honey** to the dance.

**honkey** [hʌ́ŋkiː] *n* a derogatory term for Caucasians ❺

I hate the way those **honkies** treat us.

**hood** [hud] *n* [from *neighborhood*] term for one's ❸
locale

I'm gonna head back to my **hood**, man.

**hooked** [hukt] *adj* addicted ❶

Cigarette companies want you to get **hooked**, cuz once
you're **hooked** they've got you till you die.

**hooker** [húkər] *n* prostitute, whore ❸

There's always **hookers** standing on every corner in
your neighborhood.

see also: SLUT

**hoopla** [húːplɑ] *n* celebration, excited commotion ❶

What's this **hoopla** all about? I mean, is the President
in town?

see also: HYPE, TO-DO

**horny** [hɔ́ːrniː] *adj* eager for sex ❹

When he's **horny** he tries to pick up chicks at the bar.

My girlfriend was feeling really **horny** last night. We
made love until two in the morning.

**horror show** [hɑrər ʃou] *n* a terrible situation  ❸

Man, the battlefield is a real **horror show**. There're corpses lying all over the place.

**horse around** [hɔrs əráund] *v* to engage in rough or ❶ boisterous play

OK kids, stop **horsing around**. It's time to go to bed.

see also:  CLOWN AROUND, FOOL AROUND

**hot** [hɑt] *adj* sexy  ❸

Wow, check out that **hot** babe over there in the leather mini-skirt.

see also:  FOXY

**hot rod** [hɑt rɑd] *n* a fast, cool car  ❶

Bob's got this new **hot rod**. It's the fastest thing I've ever seen.

**hot shit** [hɑt ʃít] *n* arrogant person  ❹

Tommy thinks he's such **hot shit**, but really, he's just a dweeb.

see also:  HOTSHOT

**hotshot** [hátʃat] *n* very talented or successful person  ❶

Who's the **hotshot** on the skateboard?

**hots (the)** [ðə háts] *n* sexual attraction  ❸

John's got **the hots** for Karen, but he's too shy to tell her how much he likes her.

see also:  CRUSH

**hot water** [hɑt wɔ́ːdər] *n* trouble, difficulty  ❶

You'll be in **hot water** if your parents find out.

see also:  BIND, IN DEEP SHIT, JAM, TIGHT SPOT, UP SHIT'S CREEK

**how 'bout** [haubaut] *exp* [from *how about*]  ❶

    **How 'bout** goin' to a movie tonight?

    **How 'bout** it?

    A: <u>Wanna</u> go to a movie?

    B: Yeah, <u>OK</u>.

    A: **How 'bout** you?

    C: Yeah, I <u>wanna</u> go too.

**how come?** [hau kʌ́m] *exp* "Why?"  ❶

    **How come** you never help me with the housework?

**"howdy"** [háudiː] *exp* [from *How do you do?*] "Hello"  ❶

    **Howdy**, neighbor. How's it going?

**humongous** [hjuːmáŋgis] *adj* huge  ❸

    Dinosaurs were **humongous** creatures.

**hump** [hʌmp] *v* to have sexual intercourse  ❺

    I saw two dogs **humping** in the backyard.

    see also: BANG, FUCK, LAY, MAKE LOVE, PORK, SCREW

**hung up** [hʌŋ ʌ́p] *adj* preoccupied, obsessed  ❶

    She's pretty **hung up** about the mole on her face.

**hunk** [hʌŋk] *n* a handsome, muscular man  ❶

    <u>Wow</u>, he's a <u>real</u> **hunk**. I wonder if he has any brains.

    see also: STUD, REAL MAN

**hurting** [hɚ́tiŋ] *adj* to be in pain  ❶

    He's been **hurting** pretty bad ever since his wife left him for another man.

    see also: IN A BAD WAY

**hussy** [hʌsiː] *n* a lewd girl or woman  ❸

That girl's a no-good **hussy**. Look at how she flirts with every <u>guy</u> she meets.

see also:  BIMBO, EASY RIDE, NYMPHO, SLUT

**hustle** [hʌsəl] *v* to work hard, move fast  ❶

If you want to make money in this world, you've got to **hustle**.

see also:  BOOGIE, BREAK ONE'S BALLS, BUST ONE'S BALLS, BUST ONE'S BUTT, CRANK, HAUL ASS, KNOCK ONESELF OUT

**hustle** [hʌsəl] *v* to deceive  ❶

She got **hustled** by a <u>con-man</u>.

see also:  CON, CON-MAN, HAD, SHORTCHANGE

**hype** [haip] *n* exaggerated publicity  ❶

There was <u>tons</u> of **hype** in the media about Peter's new slang dictionary.

see also:  HOOPLA, TO-DO

**hyper** [háipər] *adj* nervous, overly excited and energetic  ❸

He had to get to work, but couldn't find his keys. Boy, was he **hyper**.

<u>Chill out</u> <u>man</u>, Don't act so **hyper**.

Her kids were running around and acting **hyper**, so they all had to leave the church.

# I

**icky** [íkiː] *adj* disgusting ❷

There was some **icky** <u>stuff</u> on my sandwich, so I threw it away.

see also: GNARLY, GRODY, GROSS, YUCKY

**iffy** [ífiː] *adj* dubious, uncertain ❶

The veterinarian says it's pretty **iffy**. It looks like your dog has only a fifty percent chance of surviving.

see also: DICEY

**"I hear you"** [ai híər juː] *inter* "I sympathize with ❶ your point of view"

A: I hate school. I'm never going again.

B: **I hear you**, but you have to get an education. Tell me why you don't like it.

**"I mean..."** [ai míːn] *exp* this phrase literally means ❸ "I think" or "I feel that", but is typically used as conversational filler

You look great today. **I mean** your clothes are beautiful.

I can't believe they're going out. He's, <u>like</u>, **I mean**, <u>really</u> cute, and she's not pretty at all. **I mean**, it's <u>like</u>, <u>ya know</u>, he pities her <u>or something</u>.

see also: LIKE, YOU KNOW

**"I'm outta' here"** [aim áudə hiər] inter "I'm leaving ❸ immediately"

<u>OK</u>, **I'm outta' here**. I'm <u>gonna</u> go home and sleep.

see also: ADIOS, CIAO, LATER, SEE YA, TAKE IT EASY

123

**in** [in] *adj* fashionable ❶

Mini-skirts are **in** again, and long skirts are out.

**in a bad way** [in ə bæd wéi] *adj* in bad condition ❸

He's **in a bad way** <u>cuz</u> he can't find any <u>dope</u>.

see also: HURTING

**"in a sec"** [in ə sék] *exp* [from *in a second*] after a ❶
short time

Sorry, I'm on the other line. I'll call you back **in a sec**,
<u>OK</u>?

**in cahoots with** [in kəhúːts wiθ] *adj* in ❶
collaboration with

Some people think he's **in cahoots** with the CIA.

**in deep shit** [in diːp ʃít] *adj* in big trouble ❹

I can't believe you wrecked her car. Now you're **in deep
shit**.

see also: BIND, HOT WATER, JAM, TIGHT SPOT, UP SHIT'S CREEK

**in one's face/in your face** [in wʌnz féis] ❸
*adj* aggressive and annoying

I can't stand the way the waiters here are always **in
your face**.

Why are you always **in my face**? Get <u>outta</u> my face
<u>already</u> will <u>ya</u>?

see also: PESTY, PESKY, PUSHY

**in shape** [in seip] *adj* physically fit, healthy ❶

I <u>wanna</u> get **in shape** before summer so I'll look good
in my bikini.

see also: BUILT, CUT

**inside out** [insaidáut] *adj* in such a manner that an ❶
inner surface becomes the outer, a state of great
disarray

Your shirt is **inside out**.

The cops turned his apartment **inside out** looking for
the stolen credit cards.

**inside out** [insaidáut] *adv* completely, thoroughly ❶

Einstein knew physics **inside out**.

You'll need to know the material **inside out** if you
expect to pass the final.

**in sync** [in síŋk] *adj* synchronous ❶

Let's get our watches **in sync**.

We think the same way. We're <u>really</u> **in sync** with each
other.

**intense** [intens] *adj* extreme ❶

She has <u>real</u> **intense** eyes. When she looks at me she
makes me nervous.

I like clothes with **intense** <u>funky</u> colors.

He's a <u>really</u> **intense** person. He always wants to talk
about politics and philosophy.

He's <u>really</u> **intense** about learning Swahili. He's going to
Kenya next year.

see also: AWESOME, BAD, BADASS, CRAZY-ASS, EXCELLENT, OUT
OF SIGHT, OUT OF THIS WORLD, RAD, SUPER, TO DIE
FOR, WILD

**into (to be)** [íntu:] *adj* involved with, to be obsessed ❶
with

They're <u>really</u> **into** each other. They do everything
together: eat, work, and sleep.

He's <u>really</u> **into** his job. He loves what he does and he does it well.

see also: DIG

**"in your dreams!"** [in jər dríːmz] *inter* "Not a ❶ chance!"

A: Hey <u>girl</u>, what's your name? You're <u>gorgeous</u>. <u>Wanna</u> marry me?

B: <u>Yeah right</u>. **In your dreams!**

see also: FAT CHANCE, NO WAY, YEAH RIGHT

**IOU** [ai ou juː] *n* [from prounuciation of *I Owe You*] ❶ a document promising repayment

I don't have any money. Can I write you an **IOU**?

**"it depends"/"depends"** [it depenz, depenz] ❶ *v* "maybe"

A: Are you <u>gonna</u> go to America?

B: **It depends**.

A: **Depends** on what?

B: **It depends** on whether I can save enough money to buy a ticket.

**"it's like this"** [its laik ðís] *exp* "Let me explain the ❶ situation"

**It's like this** <u>man</u>: I need a little <u>dough</u>. Can you spare some?

**itsy-bitsy/itty-bitty** [ìtsi bítsiː, ìtiː bítiː] *adj* very ❷ small, tiny

An **itsy-bitsy** spider climbed up the water spout.

# J

**'ja** [dʒə] *contr* [from *did you*]  ❶

When**ja** go to America? = When did you go to America?

Wha**ja** do yesterday? = What did you do yesterday?

Why**ja** stop? = Why did you stop?

**jack of all trades** [dʒæk əf ɔːl tréidz] *n* person possessing many different skills

Donny's a <u>real</u> **jack of all trades**. He can fix anything.

**jack off** [dʒæk ɔːf] *v* to masturbate  ❺

That <u>guy</u> spends all of his time in the bathroom **jacking off**.

see also:  JERK OFF

**jack(shit)** [dʒæk ʃít] *n* worthless bit, nothing  ❸ ❹

That <u>guy</u> doesn't know **jack** about me.

He didn't say **jackshit** while I was there. Is he afraid of me?

see also:  DICK, DIDDLY, PEANUTS, SQUAT, ZILCH, ZIP

**jalopy** [dʒəlápiː] *n* dilapidated old vehicle  ❶

He was driving an old **jalopy** that needed a new muffler.

see also:  CLUNKER, HEAP

**jam** [dʒæm] *n* a difficult situation ❶

I'm in a bit of a **jam**. My car broke down on the highway. Can you help me?

see also: BIND, HOT WATER, IN DEEP SHIT, TIGHT SPOT, UP SHIT'S CREEK

**jam** [dʒæm] *v* to play music together ❶

We were **jammin'** in Joe's garage until the neighbors started complaining about the noise.

**jammies** [dʒǽmiːz] *n* [from *pajamas*] nightclothes ❷

Mommy, I can't find my **jammies**. Is it alright if I sleep in my underwear?

see also: PJ'S

**JAP** [dʒæp] *n* [from *Jewish American Princess*] derogatory term for a young, rich, and spoiled Jewish woman (warning: *Jap* is a very derogatory term for Japanese) ❹

There were lots of **JAPs** at the mall.

see also: PRINCESS

**jazz up** [dʒæz ʌp] *v* to enhance the brightness of, to improve ❶

He **jazzed** up his car with crazy colors.

**"jeez!"** [dʒiːz] *inter* [from *Jesus*] expression of surprise, anger, frustration ❶

**Jeez**, I can't believe how hot it is today.

see also: DAG, DANG, DARN, DRAT, GEE, GOLLY, GOOD GRIEF, GOSH, SHOOT

**jell** [dʒel] *v* to take shape, to become distinct ❶

Pete's theory began to **jell** after he completed his experiments.

**jellyfish** [dʒéliːfiʃ] *n* person lacking backbone   ❶

He does whatever his wife tells him to do. He's such a **jellyfish**.

see also: PUSHOVER, WIMP, WUSS

**jerk** [dʒərk] *n* a contemptible person   ❶

Sometimes you act like a <u>real</u> **jerk** at parties. You <u>really</u> shouldn't drink so much.

Her new boyfriend is a <u>total</u> **jerk**. I wonder what she sees in him.

see also: ASSHOLE, BASTARD, COCKSUCKER, CREEP, DICK, DICKWEED, DIP, DIPSHIT, DOUCHE BAG, FUCK, FUCKER, MOTHERFUCKER, PRICK, SCHMUCK, SOB, SON OF A BITCH

**jerk off** [dʒərk ɔːf] *v* to masturbate   ❺

He's always <u>horny</u>, but he doesn't have a girlfriend so he **jerks off** while watching <u>porno</u> videos.

see also: JACK OFF

**"Jesus Christ!"** [dʒìzis kráist] *inter* expression of anger, frustration or suprise   ❹

**Jesus Christ!** Drive more carefully! You almost hit that kid playing in the street.

see also: CHRIST, DAMN, FOR CHRISTSAKE, GOD

**jibe** [dʒaib] *v* to mesh, to match, to agree   ❶

What he told us last night just doesn't **jibe** with what his mother told me.

**jillion** [dʒíljən] *n* indeterminately large number   ❸

There are **jillions** of stars in the sky.

see also: TON, UMPTEEN, ZILLION

**jinx** [dʒiŋks] *n* a hex, a spell, a curse ❶

A: I can't believe you lost that tennis game to Jim!

B: Yeah, I think he put a **jinx** on me.

**jitters (the)** [ðə dʒítərz] *n* a state of panic or fear ❶

Walking on thin ice <u>really</u> gives me the **jitters**.

see also: CREEPS, WILLIES

**jive** [dʒaiv] *n* deceptive nonsense ❸

Politicians are always talking **jive** about how they're helping people.

see also: BALONEY, BULLSHIT, CRAP, GARBAGE, RUBBISH, TRASH

**jock** [dʒɑk] *n* a male athlete ❸

She always goes out with **jocks**. I think she's more into men's bodies than their minds.

see also STUD, HUNK, REAL MAN

**Joe Schmoe** [dʒou ʃmóu] *n* an ordinary, non-descript person ❶

Ask any **Joe Schmoe**, and he'll tell you that money makes the world go 'round.

**john** [dʒɑn] *n* toilet ❶

I've got to go to the **john**.

see also: CAN

**johnson** [dʒánsən] *n* penis ❹

He's very proud of his **johnson**.

see also: COCK, DICK, PECKER, PRICK, WEENIE, WILLY

**joint** [dʒɔint] *n* place, restaurant, bar ❶

Who's in charge of this **joint**?

see also: HANGOUT

**joint** [dʒɔint] *n* a marijuana cigarette ❸

Pass me that **joint**, will you? I want to smoke it before the show.

**joker** [dʒóukər] *n* an obnoxious or incompetent person ❶

Who's the **joker** who spilled catsup in my book?

see also: HAM

**jump all over** [dʒʌmp ɔːl óuvər] *v* to criticize ❶

Why do you have to **jump all over** him all the time? He's doing his best.

see also: BAWL SOMEONE OUT, CHEW SOMEONE OUT, COME DOWN ON SOMEONE, JUMP ON, LET SOMEONE HAVE IT, RAG ON, TAKE IT OUT ON

**jumping bean** [dʒʌ́mpiŋ biːn] *n* a lively person ❷

When she drinks coffee she's like a **jumping bean**. She can't sit still.

see also: LIVE WIRE

**jump on (one)** [dʒʌmp ɔn wʌn] *v* to criticize ❶

She <u>really</u> **jumped on him** for saying "<u>girl</u>" instead of "woman", because she thought "<u>girl</u>" was sexist.

see also: BAWL SOMEONE OUT, CHEW SOMEONE OUT, COME DOWN ON SOMEONE, JUMP ALL OVER, LET SOMEONE HAVE IT, RAG ON, TAKE IT OUT ON

**jungle** [dʒʌ́ŋgəl] *n* a dangerous and uncivilized place ❶

It's a <u>real</u> **jungle** in the city. Nobody is going to help you there except yourself.

**junk** [dʒʌŋk] *v* to discard ❶

I **junked** my car <u>cuz</u> it was <u>totally</u> <u>beat-up</u>.

**junk food** [dʒʌ́ŋk fuːd] *n* unhealthful food ❶

If you stopped eating so much **junk food** you wouldn't have so many <u>zits</u>.

**junkie** [dʒʌ́ŋkiː] *n* an addict ❶

He's not dead, just sleeping in the street. **Junkies** always do that.

see also: DOPE FIEND

**junk mail** [dʒʌ́ŋk meil] *n* advertisements that come ❶ in the mail

I always throw my **junk mail** away without reading it. I don't need useless coupons or supermarket flyers.

**"just a sec'"** [dzestəsék] *inter* [from *wait just a second*] ❶ "In a moment"

I'll be over in **just a sec'**.

**Just a sec'**. I'll be right with you.

# K

**"'K"** [kei] *inter* [from *OK*] "All right" ❶

'**K**, I'm ready. Let's go.

**kaboom!** [kəbúːm] *adv* with violent abruptness ❶

The bomb went "**kaboom!**"! It was <u>really</u> loud.

see also: BAM, BOOM, POW, WHAM

**kaput** [kəpút] *adj* broken ❶

The vending machine is **kaput** again. Better call the repairman.

see also: SHOT

**keel over** [ki:l óuvər] v to fall down suddenly, to ❶
collapse, to die

The old man just **keeled over** and died.

see also: CROAK

**keen** [ki:n] adj eager ❶

He's <u>really</u> **keen** on going to Europe. He's never been
there.

see also: GUNG HO, PSYCHED, PUMPED

**keep one's cool** [ki:p wʌnz kú:l] v to maintain ❸
one's composure

I told him to **keep his cool**. But he <u>lost it</u> and yelled at
his boss.

see also: MAINTAIN ONE'S COOL

**kick-ass** [kík æs] adj wonderful, uncompromising ❹

This is a **kick-ass** radio station. I love it.

see also: AWESOME, COOL, SUPER

**kick butt/ass** [kik bʌt/æs] v to win, to do well ❸ ❹

A: Did you win?
B: Yeah, we **kicked butt**.

**kick one's ass** [kik wʌnz æs] v to defeat decisively ❹

We **kicked their ass** in basketball today. The final
score was 131 to 65.

I'm gonna **kick your ass** <u>man</u>.

see also: CLOBBER, CREAM, CRUSH, MASSACRE, SLAUGHTER

**kick out** [kík aut] v to evict, eject ❶

I was **kicked out** of my house when I was sixteen.

see also: BOOT

**kick(s)** [kiks] *n* pleasurable experience or effect  ❶

He gets his **kicks** by torturing little animals.

He gets a **kick** out of making prank phone calls.

You should go see his play. I think you'll get a <u>real</u> **kick** out of it.

**kike** [kaik] *n* a very insulting term for a Jewish person  ❻

I can't believe you called me a **kike**!

**kill** [kil] *v* to amuse or hurt  ❸

It **kills** me when he acts like a gorilla. It's so funny.

It **kills** me to tell you this, but your application was rejected.

**killjoy** [kíldʒɔi] *n* someone who ruins the pleasure of  ❶
others

He's a **killjoy**. When he shows up at a party everyone wants to leave.

see also:  FUDDY-DUDDY, PARTY POOPER, STICK-IN-THE-MUD, WET BLANKET

**kind of/kinda'** [káind əf, káində] *adv* to some  ❶
degree

A: Do you like Chinese food?

B: **Kind of**, but my favorite is Indian.

I think she **kinda** likes me but is too shy to show it.

**kinky** [kíŋki:] *adj* sexually perverse or strange,  ❸
perverted

She's <u>really</u> **kinky** in bed.

I think he's done some **kinky** things, like have sex with three girls at the same time.

**kiss ass** [kis ǽs] *v* to curry favor ❹

Look, he's **kissing ass** again. Today he's giving the teacher an apple.

see also: BROWNNOSE, SUCK UP TO

**kisser** [kísər] *n* lips, mouth ❶

She punched him right in the **kisser**.

**klutz** [klʌts] *n* a clumsy person ❶

John is a <u>total</u> **klutz**. He's always knocking things over.

see also: PUTZ, SPAZ

**klutzy** [klʌtsi:] *adj* clumsy ❶

Dogs are pretty **klutzy** compared to cats.

He's the **klutziest** dancer I have ever met. He's always stepping on my toes.

see also: PUTZY, SPASTIC

**knock** [nɑk] *v* to criticize ❶

Hey, don't **knock** America. It has problems, but it's still a great place to live.

see also: BAD-MOUTH

**knockers** [nɑ́:kərz] *n* breasts ❹

She's got a healthy pair of **knockers**.

see also: BOOBS, TITS

**knock oneself out** [nɑk wʌnself áut] *v* to exhaust ❶
oneself

I **knocked myself out** trying to bake a cake.

see also: BREAK ONE'S BALLS, BUST ONE'S BALLS, BUST ONE'S BUTT, CRANK, HUSTLE

**knockout** [ná:kaut] *n* an extremely attractive woman ❶

Wow, that girl's a **knockout**.

see also: BABE

**know-it-all** [nóuitɔːl] *n* one who claims to know ❷
everything

She's such a **know-it-all**. She just wants to show off.

see also: SMARTY-PANTS

**"know what?"** [nou wʌt] *inter* [from *do you know* ❶
*what?*]

**Know what?** I'm pregnant.

**Know what** I'm talking about?

**knucklehead** [nʌkəlhed] *n* a stupid person ❶

He's such a **knucklehead**. He put oil in his gas tank
again!

see also: AIRHEAD, BIRDBRAIN, BLOCKHEAD, BONEHEAD, BOZO,
CRETIN, DIMWIT, DINGBAT, DITZ, DODO, DOPE,
DUMBELL, DUMMY, GOOF, GOOFBALL, LAMEBRAIN,
MEATHEAD, NINCOMPOOP, NUMBSKULL, PEA-BRAIN,
RETARD, SCATTERBRAIN, SPACE CADET, TWIT

**kook** [kuːk] *n* a strange or weird person ❶

My Aunt is a **kook**. She's always talking to herself and
thinks Martians live in her basement.

see also: BASKET CASE, FREAK, FRUITCAKE, NUTCASE, ODDBALL,
SCREWBALL, WEIRDO, WHACKO

**kooky** [kúːkiː] *adj* crazy, weird ❶

He lives in a <u>real</u> **kooky** house. It looks like it's haunted
and it's painted purple.

see also: BATTY, BONKERS, LOONEY, LOSE ONE'S MARBLES, NUTS,
OFF THE WALL, OUT IN LEFT FIELD, OUT THERE, OUT
TO LUNCH, SCREWY, WAY-OUT, WHACKO,
WHACKED-OUT, WHACKY, WHACKO

# L

**lady's man** [léidiːz mæn] *n* a man who attracts the ❶
company of women

He's a <u>real</u> **lady's man**. He loves all women and they all
love him.

   see also: DON JUAN, WOMANIZER

**laid-back** [leid bǽk] *adj* relaxed ❸

People are more **laid-back** in California than they are
in New York.

   see also: MELLOW

**lame** [leim] *adj* bad, unacceptable ❸

She said she couldn't go out with him because she had
to wash her hair. What a **lame** excuse!

He made his girlfriend wait for him for four hours.
That's so **lame**.

   see also: CRAPPY, CRUMMY, FOUL, LOUSY, SHITTY

**lamebrain** [léimbrein] *n* a dumb person ❶

Hey **lamebrain**, that's furniture polish that you're
about to drink.

   see also: AIRHEAD, BIRDBRAIN, BLOCKHEAD, BONEHEAD, BOZO,
   CRETIN, DIMWIT, DINGBAT, DITZ, DODO, DOPE,
   DUMBELL, DUMMY, GOOF, GOOFBALL, KNUCKLEHEAD,
   MEATHEAD, NINCOMPOOP, NUMBSKULL, PEA-BRAIN,
   RETARD, SCATTERBRAIN, SPACE CADET, TWIT

**latch on to** [lætʃ ɑn tuː] *v* to grasp, get hold of ❶

His followers **latched on to** every word he said.

**"later"** [léidər] *inter* [from *see you later*] "Good-bye"  ❸

Later man, I'm outta here.

see also: ADIOS, CIAO, I'M OUTTA HERE, SEE YA, TAKE IT EASY

**lay** [lei] *n* act of sexual intercourse  ❺

Man, you're so uptight! You need a good **lay**.

see also: BANG, FUCK, HUMP, SCREW

**lay** [lei] *v* to have sexual intercourse  ❺

I was sixteen when I got **laid** for the first time.

see also: BANG, FUCK, HUMP, MAKE LOVE, PORK, SCREW

**lay a fart** [lei ə fart] *v* to pass intestinal gas  ❸

Who **laid a fart**? It stinks in here.

see also: CUT THE CHEESE, FART

**lay it on one** [lei it ɔn wʌn] *v* to be honest  ❸

OK, **lay it on me**. I want the truth. Do I have cancer or not?

see also: GIVE IT TO ONE STRAIGHT, TELL IT LIKE IT IS

**lay it on thick** [lei it ɔn θik] *v* to exaggerate or overstate  ❸

He really **lays it on thick** when he flatters women, and they love it.

When my boss praised my work he **laid it on** pretty **thick**. He's hoping I won't ask for a raise now.

**lay off** [lei ɔːf] *v* to discontinue, cease  ❶

I've decided to **lay off** drinking beer until my beer belly disappears.

**lay off** [lei ɔ́ːf] *v* to dismiss someone from employment ❶

I was **laid off** last week even though I've worked at the company for twenty-five years.

see also: GET THE AXE, SACK

**"lay off!"** [lei ɔ́ːf] *imp* "Stop doing that!" ❶

**Lay off** or I'll call the cops!

<u>Mom</u>, would you please **lay off**? I'll do my homework after dinner.

see also: BUG OFF

**lefty** [léftiː] *n* person who is left-handed ❶

Some people think that **lefties** are naturally more creative.

Are you a **lefty**?

**legalese** [liːgəlíːz] *n* specialized language of the legal ❶
profession

The contract was written in **legalese** so confusing even my lawyer had trouble with it.

see also: GOBBLEDYGOOK

**legit** [lədʒít] *adj* [from *legitimate*] valid ❶

Your excuse for being late had better be **legit**, or you'll be fired.

**lemme** [lémiː] *contr* [from *let me*] ❶

**Lemme** go! You're hurting me!

**Lemme** see. <u>C'mon</u>, it's my turn to use the binoculars.

**lemon** [lémin] *n* a unreliable car or appliance ❶

I think I bought a **lemon**. My car's only two weeks old, but it's already in the shop.

see also: CLUNKER, HEAP

**letdown** [létdaun] *n* a disappointment ❶

It was a real **letdown** to hear I had failed the test.

see also: BUMMER, DOWNER

**let it all hang out** [let it ɔːl hæŋ áut] *v* to be ❸
completely candid, honest, relaxed

People were **letting it all hang** out last night at the
group therapy meeting.

**let it go** [let it góu] *v* to release one's hold ❶

Hey man, you can't hate him forever. You have got to
**let it go**.

**let it slide** [let it sláid] *v* to allow something to be ❶
ignored

I knew she was stealing from me, but I **let it slide**
because I was in love with her.

see also: BLOW OFF

**let one down** [let wʌn dáun] *v* to fail to support, to ❶
disappoint

You really **let him down** when you failed to deliver
your manuscript on time.

Don't worry, I won't **let you down**.

**let someone have it** [let sʌmwʌn hæv it] *v* to ❶
criticize severely

I'm gonna really **let her have it** when she gets here.

My boss really **let me have it** for getting to work late
again.

see also: BAWL SOMEONE OUT, CHEW SOMEONE OUT, COME
DOWN ON SOMEONE, JUMP ALL OVER, JUMP ON, RAG
ON, TAKE IT OUT ON

**let up** [let ʌp] *v* to stop entirely, cease ❶

The rain's finally **letting up**.

**level** [lévəl] *v* be frank and open ❶

**Level** with me, <u>OK</u>? Did you steal the money or not?

**lick** [lik] *v* to defeat ❶

We're going to **lick** their football team!

see also: CLOBBER, CREAM, CRUSH, KICK ONE'S ASS, MASSACRE, SLAUGHTER

**life of the party** [laif ɔf ðə párdi:] *n* a lively, ❶
amusing person

He is always the **life of the party**. He loves to make everybody laugh.

**lifesaver** [láifseivər] *n* someone who rescues a person ❶
or situation

Thanks for walking me home through this dangerous neighborhood. You're a **lifesaver**.

**lighten up** [laitən ʌp] *v* to relax, be less serious ❶

Why don't you **lighten up** a little? You're scaring the kids.

see also: CHILL, TAKE IT EASY

**like** [laik] conversational filler ❸

He's **like**, the cutest guy in the school. **Like**, all the <u>girls</u> are **like** crazy about him.

see also: I MEAN, YOU KNOW

**like mad/crazy** [laik mǽd, krḗizi:] *adv* without ❶
restraint, with great enthusiasm

She loves him **like mad**.

She studies English **like crazy** three or four hours a day.

**like it's going out of style** [laik its gouiŋ audəv stáil] *adv* with enthusiasm or speed ❶

She buys shoes **like they're going out of style**.

He spends money **like it's going out of style**.

see also: LIKE MAD

**line** [lain] *n* a deceptive story, a lie ❶

He's always giving me some **line** about why he needs a few dollars.

see also: STORY

**lip** [lip] *n* back talk ❶

You give me any more of your **lip**, and I won't let you use the car.

see also: FRESH, TALK BACK

**lip service** [líp sərvis] *n* insincere expression of ❶
agreement or support

Even though he doesn't believe in God he pays **lip service** to the church, <u>cuz</u> he wants to keep his parents happy.

**litterbug** [lídərbʌg] *n* someone who disposes of ❶
trash or garbage carelessly

What are you, a **litterbug**? Don't throw trash on the ground.

**live large** [liv lardʒ] *v* to enjoy an extravagant ❸
lifestyle

Even though he <u>ain't</u> got much money he likes to **live large**.

**live wire** [láiv waijər] *n* an energetic person ❶

I can't believe your <u>mom's</u> seventy! She's such a **live wire**.

see also: JUMPING BEAN

**loaded** [lóudəd] *adj* very wealthy ❶

<u>Wow</u>, look how large their house is. They must be **loaded**.

see also: STINKING RICH

**"long time, no see"** [lɔːŋ taim nou síː] *exp* ❶
"It's been a long time since we last met"

**Long time, no see**, Jim. How've <u>ya</u> been?

**lookout** [lúkaut] *n* person who keeps watch ❶

All the <u>dope</u> <u>pushers</u> cleared out, <u>cuz</u> their **lookout** told them that the <u>cops</u> were coming.

**looney** [lúːniː] *adj* crazy, eccentric ❷

He's <u>really</u> **looney**. He thinks he can hear angels singing.

see also: BATTY, BONKERS, KOOKY, NUTS, OFF THE WALL, OUT IN LEFT FIELD, OUT THERE, OUT TO LUNCH, SCREWY, WAY-OUT, WHACKO, WHACKED-OUT, WHACKY, WHACKO

**loose** [luːs] *adj* sexually promiscuous ❸

From what I hear she's pretty **loose**. You'll have no trouble getting <u>laid</u> tonight.

see also: EASY RIDE, SKANKY, SLUTTY

**lose it** [lúːz it] *v* to lose self control ❶

He **lost it** when she told him she was leaving him for his best friend.

see also: BLOW A HAIRY, BLOW ONE'S COOL, FLIP, FREAK, GO APESHIT, GO BANANAS, GO POSTAL, LOSE ONE'S COOL

**lose one's cool** [luːz wʌnz kúːl] v to lose one's self ❶ control, to get angry

He **lost his cool** when his dad said he couldn't use the car. He cursed at him and then ran out of the house.

see also: BLOW A HAIRY, BLOW ONE'S COOL, FLIP, FREAK, GO APESHIT, GO BANANAS, GO POSTAL, LOSE IT

**lose one's marbles** [luːz wʌnz márbəlz] v to lose ❶ one's sanity

He **lost his marbles** after smoking too much <u>pot</u>.

see also: GO BONKERS, GO NUTS

**lose out on** [luːz áut ɔn] v to miss an opportunity ❶

He **lost out on** the chance to go to Harvard because he missed the interview.

see also: BLOW IT, MISS THE BOAT

**loser** [lúːzər] n one who is incompetent or unable to ❶ succeed

He's a <u>real</u> **loser**. He's never had a job for more than two months because he shows up to work drunk and fights with the other workers.

see also: BUM, LOWLIFE

**lousy** [láuziː] adj inferior, bad, repulsive ❶

I'm tired of driving this **lousy** car. I'm <u>gonna</u> get a new one.

I'm feeling pretty **lousy** today. I think I'm getting my period.

see also: CRAPPY, CRUMMY, FOUL, LAME, SHITTY

**lovey** [lʌ́viː] exp term of endearment ❶

Hey **lovey**, come sit down next to me.

see also: BABY, HONEY, SWEETIE

**lovey-dovey** [lʌviː dʌviː] *adj* extremely affectionate ❶

They're always **lovey-dovey** when they make up after a fight.

see also:  MUSHY

**low-down** [lóu daun] *adj* contemptible ❶

Who's the **low-down** idiot who stole my bike?

It's pretty **low-down** to kill a puppy.

see also:  DAMN, FUCKING, LAME, SHITTY

**lowlife** [lóulaif] *n* a person of low character or social ❶ status

That guy is not your friend. He's a **lowlife** who will use you.

see also:  BUM, LOSER

**luck into** [lʌk íntuː] *v* to happen upon something ❶ good by chance

He **lucked into** some money and bought an airplane ticket to Nepal with it.

see also:  HIT THE JACKPOT

**luck out** [lʌk áut] *v* to gain something desirable ❶ through good fortune

I can't believe the teacher lost the tests. We <u>really</u> **lucked out** because I know I failed it.

**lucky dog** [lʌkiː dɔ́ːg] *n* a person who is very ❶ fortunate

You **lucky dog**, I can't believe you won the lottery!

**lush** [lʌʃ] *n* a drunkard ❶

Her husband's a **lush**. She thinks that she can change him, but the odds are against her.

see also: WINO

# M

**mad about** [mæd əbaut] *adj* very fond of or infatuated with ❶

She's **mad about** Jimmy.

see also: CRAZY ABOUT

**mad dog** [mæd dɔːg] *n* a violent or crazy person ❶

That <u>dude's</u> a **mad dog**. He'll beat up anybody who makes him angry.

see also: PSYCHO

**main drag** [mein dræg] *n* the principal street of a city ❸

They were <u>cruising</u> up and down the **main drag**.

**maintain one's cool** [meintein wʌnz kúːl] *v* to keep one's composure ❶

<u>Man</u>, in life you gotta **maintain your cool**, or else you'll get yourself into some deep <u>shit</u>.

see also: KEEP ONE'S COOL

**major** [méidʒər] *adj* extreme, serious ❶

There's <u>gonna</u> be a **major** party this weekend at John's place.

I made a **major** mistake when I turned down that job.

see also:  BIG-TIME, HUMONGOUS, REAL

**make a stink** [meik ə stíŋk] v to complain loudly   ❶

Every time she goes to a restaurant she **makes a stink** about the service and embarrasses the hell out of me.

see also:  BITCH, GRIPE, SOUND OFF, START SHIT, RAISE HELL

**make it** [méik it] v to succeed, win acceptance   ❶

I want to **make it** as a writer.

**make it** [méik it] v to meet a deadline or   ❶
appointment

I'm not going to **make it** today. Let's reschedule for tomorrow.

**make like** [méik laik] v to pretend, behave as if   ❶

He was **making like** he was asleep, but I knew he was awake.

see also:  FAKE IT

**make love** [meik lʌv] v to have sex   ❶

Somebody was **making love** in the next room. I could hear everything.

see also:  BANG, FUCK, HUMP, PORK, SCREW

**make out** [meik áut] v to kiss passionately, engage   ❸
in sexual foreplay

They were **making out** in the back of the car.

see also:  FOOL AROUND, NECK, PET, SCREW AROUND, SMOOCH

**make out** [meik aut] v to determine, to discern with   ❶
difficulty

Can you **make out** what the sign says from here?

**make out** [meik aut] v to fare, manage ❶

How's your brother **making out** at his new job?

see also:  COPE, DEAL WITH, GET BY

**mama's boy** [mámɑz bɔi] n a man or boy who is ❶
excessively attached to his mother

He's forty-three and still he calls his mother everyday.
What a **mama's boy**.

**"man!"** [mæn] inter expression of anger, frustration ❸
or surprise, also as a term of address

**Man**, it's as hot as hell today!

Hey **man**, how ya doin'?

C'mon **man**, don't lie to me. Give it to me straight.

**Man**, you have got to be kidding. Who do you think
you are?

see also:  BUD, DUDE, GUY

**massacre** [mǽsəkər] v to be resoundingly defeated, ❶
killed

We were **massacred** thirty to nothing.

see also:  CLOBBER, CREAM, CRUSH, KICK BUTT, LICK,
SLAUGHTER, WASTE

**mean** [mi:n] adj effective, excellent ❶

That's a **mean** bike you've got there.

see also:  BADASS, COOL, SLICK

**meany** [mí:ni:] n a mean or nasty person ❷

My dad is such a **meany**. He always makes me do my
homework before I can go out and play.

**measly** [mizli:] *adj* small and insignificant ❶

He paid me a **measly** dollar for my painting.

see also:  MICKEY MOUSE, RINKY-DINK

**meathead** [míːthed] *n* a stupid person ❶

Hey **meathead**, your car is blocking my driveway!

see also:  AIRHEAD, BIRDBRAIN, BLOCKHEAD, BONEHEAD, BOZO,
CRETIN, DIMWIT, DINGBAT, DITZ, DODO, DOPE,
DUMBELL, DUMMY, GOOF, GOOFBALL, KNUCKLEHEAD,
LAMEBRAIN, NINCOMPOOP, NUMBSKULL, PEA-BRAIN,
RETARD, SCATTERBRAIN, SPACE CADET, TWIT

**mega-** [mégə] *adj* great or large, greatly exceeding ❸
others of its kind

He's working on Wall Street and making **mega**-bucks.

Their album was a **mega**-hit.

see also:  MOTHER OF ALL

**mellow** [mélou] *adj* soft and relaxing ❶

She likes **mellow** music, not that <u>garbage</u> the kids
listen to.

see also:  LAID-BACK

**mensch** [mentʃ] *n* a person of integrity and honor ❶

I saw him helping an old lady across the street. He's
such a **mensch**.

**mess** [mes] *n* person in a bad emotional or physical ❶
condition

She's been a <u>total</u> **mess** ever since she got divorced. I'm
afraid she might do something crazy like commit
suicide or something.

<u>Man</u>, you are a **mess**. Were you out drinking all night
again?

see also:  WRECK

**mess (around) with** [mes aráund wiθ] *v* to ❶
experiment with, interfere with, bother

Everyone was **messing around with** different drugs in the 60's.

If you **mess with** him you're <u>gonna</u> answer to me, so watch out.

see also: DICK AROUND, FOOL WITH, FUCK WITH

**messed up** [mest ʌp] *adj* confused and unhappy ❶

John's <u>really</u> **messed up**. He's always talking about killing himself.

see also: FUCKED UP, SCREWED UP

**mess up** [més ʌp] *v* to make a big mess, make a ❶
serious mistake

He **messed up** his room just to make his <u>mom</u> mad.

You <u>really</u> **messed up** this time, my friend.

see also: SCREW UP

**Mickey Mouse** [miki: máus] *adj* insignificant, petty ❸

I'm not going to work for that **Mickey Mouse** company. It has no future.

see also: RINKY-DINK

**mind-blowing/-boggling** [máind blouiŋ, bagliŋ] ❸
*adj* amazing, overwhelming

That performance was **mind-blowing**. It was the best piano playing I've ever heard.

The sheer number of species on earth is **mind-boggling**.

see also: UNREAL

**miss the boat** [mis ðə bóut] *exp* to miss an ❶
opportunity

You'd better get those entrance applications in by the
deadline or you'll **miss the boat**!

see also:  BLOW IT, LOSE OUT ON

**"mmm-mm!"** [ə́m əm] *exp* sound one makes when ❶
something tastes or smells good

**Mmm-mm!** That soup smells delicious.

**mom** [mɑm] *n* [from *momma*] mother, ❶
term of address

My **mom** works the night shift.

**Mom**, could you wake me up early tomorrow?

see also:  MOMMY, OLD LADY

**mommy** [mámi:] *n* mother, term of address ❷

**Mommy**, I'm scared of the dark.

see also:  MOM

**monkey business** [mʌŋki: bíznes] *n* illegal or ❶
immoral activities

I don't know what's going on, but I'll bet he's involved
in some sort of **monkey business**.

see also:  RACKET, SCAM

**moola** [mú:lə] *n* money ❶

Got any **moola**? I'm broke.

see also:  BREAD, DOUGH

**moon** [mu:n] *v* to display one's buttocks as a form of ❶
insult

The boys in the back of the bus **mooned** us out the rear
window.

**mope** [moup] *v* to be depressed and dejected ❶

She's been **moping** around the house ever since she was fired.

**"mornin'"** [mɔ́rnin] *inter* [from *good morning*] ❶

**Mornin'** John, nice weather we're having isn't it?

**morning person** [mɔ́rniŋ pə̀rsən] *n* a person who ❶ is active early in the morning

I wish I was a **morning person**. I always feel sleepy and irritable until noon.

see also: NIGHT-OWL

**mother** [mʌ́ðər] *n* something particularly ❸ contemptible, impressive or difficult

It was a real **mother** trying to get that fridge out of the basement.

**motherfucker** [mʌ̀ðərfʌ́kər] *n* a contemptible person ❺

Fuck you, **motherfucker**!

Go fuck yourself, you **motherfucker**!

The new manager is a real **motherfucker**. He treats all the employees like his personal slaves.

see also: ASSHOLE, BASTARD, COCKSUCKER, CREEP, DICK, DICKWEED, DIP, DIPSHIT, DOUCHE BAG, FUCK, FUCKER, JERK, PRICK, SCHMUCK, SOB, SON OF A BITCH

**mother of all** [mʌ́ðər əv ɔːl] *adj* the best or greatest ❹ of a type

That was the **mother of all** picnics. There were, like, five hundred guests.

see also: MEGA-

**motormouth** [móudər mauθ] *n* someone who
talks incessantly ❶

My sister's a <u>real</u> **motormouth**. She's always on the
phone.

   see also: BLAB, BIG-MOUTH, GAB, YAK

**Mr. Right** [mistər rait] *n* the ideal man to marry, the ❶
best man for the job

I've been waiting a long time for **Mr. Right** to come
along.

**mug** [mʌg] *v* to assault, usually with intent to rob ❶

He was **mugged** by a gang in Central Park. They even
took his sunglasses.

**mug** [mʌg] *n* a person's face ❹

<u>God</u>, that <u>dude's</u> got an ugly **mug**.

**munchies** [mʌntʃiːz] *n* snack foods ❸

Do you have any **munchies**? I'm starving.

   see also: CHOW, GRUB

**munchies (the)** [ðə mʌntʃiːz] *n* hunger pangs ❸

I've got **the munchies**. Do you have any food in your
house?

**mushy** [mʌʃiː] *adj* excessively sentimental and ❷
romantic

I hate **mushy** movies with kissing and <u>stuff</u>.

   see also: LOVEY-DOVEY

**mutt** [mʌt] *n* a mongrel dog ❶

That dog's a **mutt**, not a golden retriever.

**"my man"** [mai mæn] *inter* "my friend"  ❸

How you doin' **my man**. <u>Whassup</u>?

# N

**nah/naw** [naː, nɔː] *adv* [from *no*]  ❶

A: You hungry?

B: **Nah**, I just ate.

see also:  NOPE, UH-UH

**nail** [neil] *v* to strike a target, to apprehend or expose  ❸

He threw a rock at the dog that was chasing him and **nailed** it in the head.

He tried to cheat on the test, but the teacher **nailed** him.

see also:  SNAG

**natural** [nætʃərul] *n* someone who has great talent or skills  ❶

He's a **natural** on the saxaphone. He was playing jazz when he was only four.

**natural-born** [nætʃərul bɔrn] *adj* innate  ❶

That <u>guy's</u> a **natural-born** killer. He has no conscience.

**nauseating** [nɔ́ːziːeidiŋ] *adj* disgusting, sickening  ❶

I think his sexism is **nauseating**.

see also:  GNARLY, GRODY, GROSS, ICKY, YUCKY

**neat** [niːt] *adj* nice, admirable  ❶

<u>Wow</u> Jimmy, where'd you get that bike? It's <u>really</u> **neat**.

see also:  COOL, SLICK

**neck** [nek] *v* to kiss passionately  ❸

Couples were **necking** on every bench in the park.

see also:  MAKE OUT, SMOOCH

**nerd** [nərd] *n* an unfashionable or socially inept  ❶
person

How come the only guys who like me are **nerds**? What
am I, a **nerd** magnet?

see also:  DORK, DRIP, DWEEB, GEEK

**nerdy** [nɚ́diː] *adj* boring, unfashionable  ❶

She likes **nerdy** guys because they're usually smart and
funny.

see also:  SQUARE

**nerve** [nərv] *n* self-assurance, boldness  ❶

She has a lot of **nerve**. How can she ask you to marry
her just so she can get a visa?

You've got **nerve** calling me at three in the morning like
that!

see also:  BALLS, CHUTZPAH, GUTS

**nice and...** [nais ən] *adv* very  ❶

I like my bath **nice and** hot.

Can you cook something **nice and** spicy?

**nickel and dime** [nikəl ən dáim] *adj* small-time,  ❶
involving a small amount of money

When I open my restaurant it won't be a **nickel and
dime** kind of place. It'll be beautiful.

see also:  DINKY, MICKEY MOUSE, RINKY-DINK

**nigger** [nígər] *n* an extremely insulting term for ❻
African-Americans; sometimes used as a term of
address between blacks

A: His girlfriend left him for a **nigger**.

B: You're such a racist! You make me sick.

**"night"/"g'night"** [nait, gənáit] *inter* [from *good* ❶
*night*]

**Night** <u>man</u>, I'll see you tomorrow.

    see also:  NIGHTY-NIGHT

**night owl** [náit aul] *n* a person who is active late at ❶
night

He's a <u>real</u> **night owl**. He writes all night and sleeps all
day.

    see also:  MORNING PERSON

**"nighty-night"/"night-night"** [naiti: náit, ❷
náit nait] *inter* [from *good night*]

**Night-night**. Sleep tight. Don't let the bed bugs bite.

    see also:  NIGHT

**nincompoop** [nínkʌmpu:p] *n* fool or simpleton ❷

Bobby's such a **nincompoop**.

    see also:  AIRHEAD, BIRDBRAIN, BLOCKHEAD, BONEHEAD, BOZO,
                CRETIN, DIMWIT, DINGBAT, DITZ, DODO, DOPE,
                DUMBELL, DUMMY, GOOF, GOOFBALL, KNUCKLEHEAD,
                LAMEBRAIN, MEATHEAD, NUMBSKULL, PEA-BRAIN,
                RETARD, SCATTERBRAIN, SPACE CADET, TWIT

**nitpick** [nít pik] *v* to engage in petty criticism ❶

She **nitpicks** her student's essays to death.

**nitpicky** [nít piki:] *adj* unjustified, small-minded, ❶
petty

She asked the speaker all kinds of **nitpicky** questions.

**nitty-gritty** [nídi: gridi:] *n* specific practical details  ❶

After a half hour of small talk they finally got down to the **nitty-gritty** of the job.

**"no biggie"** [nou bígi:] *exp* [from *It's not a big*  ❶
*problem"* or *"Don't worry about it"*]

A: I'm so sorry I made you wait out here for an hour.

B: **No biggie**. I've been reading this new book.

see also: NO PROBLEM

**nobody** [nóubadi:] *n* a person of no influence or  ❶
consequence

He looks like a **nobody**, but is actually one of the richest men in Japan.

Van Gogh was treated like a **nobody** all his life. He became famous only after he died.

see also: JOE SCHMOE, LOSER

**no class** [nou klǽs] *adj* lacking in manners or style  ❶

That guy's got **no class**. I can't believe he called his girl a bitch in front of his friends.

**no-no** [nou nou] *n* something that is forbidden  ❷

Matches are a **no-no**. You might burn the house down.

**nooky** [núki:] *n* sexual intercourse  ❸

I hear the boss was getting a little **nooky** on the side.

see also: HANKY-PANKY

**"no pain, no gain"** [nou péin nou géin] *exp*  ❸
"without effort you will not succeed"

A: I don't feel like working out at the gym today.

B: C'mon, ya gotta go. Otherwise you won't get stronger. Remember, **"no pain, no gain."**

**nope** [noup] *adv* [from *no*]  ❶
A: Did you kiss her yet?
B: **Nope**, not yet.

see also: NAH, UH-UH

**"no prob/problem"** [nou práb, prábləm] *exp*  ❸
[from *it's not a problem*] "there is no difficulty"
A: Sorry I can't make it to your party tonight.
B: **No prob**; maybe next time.

A: Do you mind if I smoke?
B: **No problem**. Go ahead.

A: I'm <u>really</u> sorry I'm late. I missed the train.
B: **No problem**. I just got here myself.

see also: NO BIGGIE

**nosey** [nóuziː] *adj* prying or inquisitive  ❶

My Aunt is so **nosey**, it <u>kills</u> me. Every time I call her she asks about my love life.

**"no shit!"** [nou ʃít] *inter* "You're kidding!" "Are you  ❹
serious?"
A: Guess what? I'm <u>gonna</u> get married next month.
B: **No shit**. I didn't even know you were <u>going out</u> with anybody.

see also: GET OUT OF HERE, YEAH RIGHT

**"no sweat"** [nou swét] *inter* "Don't worry"  ❶
A: Do you think you can drive the car in this snowstorm?
B: **No sweat**. I have lots of experience driving in the snow.

see also: NO BIGGIE, NO PROB/PROBLEM

**not!** [nɑt] *inter* [from *absolutely not!*] a sarcastic ❸
response to a leading question

A: Oh, she's <u>really</u> attractive!

B: Are you serious? You <u>really</u> think so?

A: **Not!**

**not too swift** [nɑt tuː swíft] *adj* stupid, dull witted ❶

He may be <u>good-looking</u>, but he's **not too swift**.

see also: RETARDED

**"no way!"** [nou wéi] *inter* "Absolutely not!" ❶
"Impossible!"

A: Do you love her?

B: **No way!** I don't even like her.

A: I heard that John died in a car accident last year.

B: **No way!** I saw him at a party last night.

**"no way, Jose!"** [nou wéi houzéi] *inter* "Absolutely ❶
not!"

A: <u>Wanna</u> try this?

B: **No way, Jose!** I am not going to try that soup. It
looks like <u>puke</u>.

see also: NO WAY

**nowhere** [nóuwɛər] *adj* ordinary, uninteresting, ❶
remote

I can't live in some boring, **nowhere** town. I <u>gotta</u> live
in New York City

**nowhere** [nóuwɛər] *n* a non-existent or obscure place ❶

Look, there aren't any houses or people. We're <u>really</u> in
the middle of **nowhere**.

I feel like I'm going **nowhere** in my career and it's
<u>pissing</u> me <u>off</u>.

**no-win situation** [nou win sitʃjuːéiʃən] *n* a ❶
situation certain to end in failure or disappointment

I'm in a **no-win** situation. If I don't have an abortion I
will have a baby I can't raise because I have no money
and no husband. But if I do have an abortion I will kill
my own child. What should I do?

**nuke** [nuːk] *v* [from *nuclear*] to utterly destroy with ❸
nuclear weapons

Terrorists would love to **nuke** the United Nations
building in New York.

**nuke** [nuːk] *v* [from *nuclear*] to heat food in a ❶
microwave oven

I don't feel like cooking tonight. Let's just **nuke** some
leftovers.

**number** [nʌmbər] *n* an outfit, a woman ❸

She was wearing a cute little **number** made of silk.

His new girlfriend is a <u>real</u> <u>hot</u> **number**.

**numbskull** [nʌ́mskʌl] *n* one who is stupid, ❶
dull-witted

I don't know why she's going out with him. He's such a
**numbskull**.

see also: AIRHEAD, BIRDBRAIN, BLOCKHEAD, BONEHEAD, BOZO,
CRETIN, DIMWIT, DINGBAT, DITZ, DODO, DOPE,
DUMBELL, DUMMY, GOOF, GOOFBALL, KNUCKLEHEAD,
LAMEBRAIN, MEATHEAD, NINCOMPOOP, PEA-BRAIN,
RETARD, SCATTERBRAIN, SPACE CADET, TWIT

**nut/nutcase** [nʌt, nʌ́tkeis] *n* a crazy or eccentric ❶
person

Mr. Smith is a real **nut**. He thinks he can speak to
ghosts.

see also: BASKET CASE, FREAK, FRUITCAKE, KOOK, ODDBALL,
SCREWBALL, WEIRDO, WHACKO

**nuts/nutty** [nʌtz, nʌ́tiː] *adj* crazy, eccentric ❶

I think he's **nuts**. Only a crazy person would try to canoe around Japan.

That's the **nuttiest** idea I ever heard.

see also: BATTY, BONKERS, KOOKY, LOONEY, OFF THE WALL, OUT IN LEFT FIELD, OUT THERE, OUT TO LUNCH, SCREWY, WAY-OUT, WHACKO, WHACKED-OUT, WHACKY, WHACKO

**nympho/nymphomaniac** [nímfou, nimfouméiniːæk] *n* a woman who has excessive sexual desires ❹

He said he needs a girl who's a **nympho**, <u>cuz</u> he's such a <u>sex fiend</u>.

see also: BIMBO, EASY RIDE, HUSSY, SEX FIEND, SLUT

# O

**OD** [ou diː] *v* [from *overdose*] to exceed the recommended dose ❶

All Janis' fans were shocked when they heard that she had **OD'd** on heroin.

**oddball** [ádbɔːl] *n* strange or eccentric person ❶

Don't hide in your room when the party starts. Our guests will think that you're an **oddball**.

see also: BASKET CASE, FREAK, FRUITCAKE, KOOK, NUTCASE, SCREWBALL, WEIRDO, WHACKO

**off the hook** [ɔf ðə húk] *adv* released from obligation or blame ❶

We thought you had committed the crime, but since someone else confessed, you're **off the hook**.

**off the hook** [ɔf ðə húk] *adv* a telephone receiver   ❶
placed off the cradle so that it will not ring

She took the phone **off the hook** so she could get some
sleep.

**off the wall** [ɔf ðə wɔ́ːl] *adj* weird, bizarre   ❶

When we were talking about evolution, one of the
students made a <u>real</u> **off the wall** comment. He said
that Darwin was wrong because angels did not have to
evolve, they have always just existed. What a <u>weirdo</u>!

see also:  BATTY, BONKERS, KOOKY, LOONEY, NUTS, OUT IN LEFT
FIELD, OUT THERE, OUT TO LUNCH, SCREWY, WAY-OUT,
WHACKED-OUT, WHACKO, WHACKY

**"oh my God!"** [ou mai gá:d] *inter* expression of   ❶
concern, surprise or frustration

Look, that building is on fire! **Oh my God!** There are
people on the roof!

**oh-oh** [ɔ́ ou] *inter* expression of bad news or an   ❶
unwelcome development

**Oh-oh**. Here comes a police car.

see also:  OOPS

**"okey-dokey"** [ouki: dóuki:] *inter* expression of   ❷
consent, "OK"

A:  Please bring me the peanut butter.

B:  **Okey-dokey**.

**old bag** [ould bǽg] *n* an unattractive old woman   ❹

That **old bag** constantly complains about the noise in
the library.

see also:  BATTLE-AX, BITCH

**old fart** [ould fárt] *n* disrespectful term for an old man ❸

He's only thirty but he already acts like an **old fart**.

see also: GEEZER

**oldie** [ouldi:] *n* an old song, usually from the '50s and '60s ❶

Let's listen to some **oldies**. They don't write songs like that anymore.

**old lady** [ould léidi:] *n* disrespectful term for mother or wife ❶

I <u>gotta</u> go. My **old lady** wants me home for supper.

see also: MOM

**old man** [ould mǽn] *n* father ❶

How's your **old man** doing?

I have to ask my **old man** if I can borrow the keys to the car.

see also: DAD, POP

**on a mission (from God)** [ɔn ə mìʃin frʌm gád] ❸
*exp* a sarcastic expression describing the urgency of a goal

We're **on a mission from God**. We've got to find some dates for the prom.

**on a roll** [ɔn ə roul] *exp* an abundance or string of successes ❶

The Yankees are **on a roll**. They've won ten games in a row.

Jim was **on a roll** last night. He was the <u>life of the party</u>. It was one funny joke after another.

**one and only** [wʌn ən óunli:] *n* one's only love ❶

I have no interest in other girls. Sharon is my **one and only**.

**one night stand** [wʌn nait stǽnd] *n* short term ❸
sexual relationship

I'm sick of **one night stands**. I want a long term
relationship, not just sex.

> see also: FLING

**one-on-one** [wʌn ɔn wʌn] *adv* direct encounter ❶
between two persons

I want to debate him **one-on-one**.

**one-track mind** [wʌn træk maind] *n* a mind that ❶
is limited to one line of thought

All that <u>dude</u> thinks about is sex, sex, sex. He's got a
**one-track mind**.

**on one's back/case** [ɔn wʌnz bǽk, keis] ❶
*adv* harassing, criticizing

My boss has been **on my case** all morning. First he said
my clothes were dirty. Then he told me I wasn't
working fast enough. Now he tells me that the coffee I
made is bitter.

My mom has been **on my back** for a week now to clean
up my room.

**on someone (to be)** [tu: bi: ɔn sʌ́mwʌn] *adv* at ❶
one's expense

Dinner's **on me**. You can pay next time.

**on the rag** [ɔn ðə rǽg] *adj* having one's period ❹

My girlfriend's **on the rag** and she's in a bad mood, so
watch out.

**on the rocks** [ɔn ðə rɑ́ks] *adj* ruined or spoiled ❶

Their marriage is **on the rocks**. They're going to see a
counselor next week.

**on the rocks** [ɔn ðə ráks] *adv* served over ice ❶

I'll have a scotch **on the rocks**, please.

**on the side** [ɔn ðə sáid] *adv* inconspicuously, ❶
surreptitiously

He makes some money **on the side** by doing odd jobs.

**on (to be)** [tu: bi: ɔ́n] *adj* using or showing the ❸
effects of using drugs

Are you **on** crack again? You're acting crazy.

**on (to be)** [tu: bi: ɔ́n] *adv* to perform at a high level ❶

His sense of humor was <u>really</u> **on** tonight.

<u>God</u>, the band played well. They were <u>really</u> **on** tonight.

**"oops!"** [u:ps] *inter* expression of surprise or dismay ❶

**Oops**, I dropped my fork.

**Oops**, I'm sorry. I didn't mean to bump into you.

see also: OH-OH

**open** [óupən] *adj* open-minded, tolerant, free-thinking ❶

You're not being **open** to what I'm saying.

She has a real sunny, **open** personality.

**"or something"** [ɔr sʌ́mθiŋ] *exp* expression of ❸
uncertainty

I think he went to the store **or something**.

**"ouch!"** [autʃ] *inter* expression of sudden pain ❶

**Ouch**! Don't touch my shoulders. They're <u>really</u>
sunburned.

**out cold** [aut kould] *adj* unconscious, asleep    ❶

He fell asleep in the street. The cops tried to wake him, but he was **out cold**.

**out in/of left field** [aut in, ʌv left fiːld] *adj* crazy,    ❶
not in touch with reality

I think he's <u>lost his marbles</u>. He's <u>really</u> **out in left field**.

His comments were **out of left field**.

see also:   BATTY, BONKERS, KOOKY, LOONEY, NUTS, OFF THE WALL, OUT THERE, OUT TO LUNCH, SCREWY, WAY-OUT, WHACKED-OUT, WHACKO, WHACKY

**out of control** [aut ʌv kintróul] *adj* uncontrollable,    ❶
unruly

Mrs. Smith, your boy is **out of control**. He keeps spitting on everybody in the classroom.

**out of it** [áudəvit] *adj* tired, confused, disoriented    ❶

I think I'm getting a cold <u>or something</u>. I feel <u>really</u> **out of it**.

see also:   BEAT, BLEARY-EYED, BURNED OUT, BUSHED, DEAD, FRAZZLED, FRIED, POOPED, WASTED, WIPED OUT, ZONKED OUT

**out of shape** [audəv ʃéip] *adj* in poor condition    ❶

I haven't exercised all winter. I feel <u>really</u> **out of shape**.

**"out of sight!"/"outta sight!"** [audəv sáit,    ❸
autəsáit] *inter* "Fantastic!"

**Outta sight!** I got an "A" on my test!

see also:   AWESOME, DYNAMITE, EXCELLENT, FAR OUT, GREAT, OUT OF SIGHT, RIGHT ON, WOW

**out of sight/outta sight** [audəv sáit, autəsáit]   ❸
*adj* excellent, superb

<u>Man</u>, that <u>girl</u> in the bikini is **out of sight**. What a <u>bod</u>!

see also:  AWESOME, BAD, BADASS, CRAZY-ASS, EXCELLENT,
INTENSE, OUT OF THIS WORLD, RAD, SUPER, TO DIE
FOR, WILD

**out of this world** [audəv ðis wə́rld]   ❶
*adj* extraordinary, superb

Her cooking is **out of this world**. You'll love it.

see also:  AWESOME, BAD, BADASS, CRAZY-ASS, EXCELLENT,
INTENSE, OUT OF SIGHT, RAD, SUPER, TO DIE FOR, WILD

**out there** [áut ðɛər] *adj* strange, weird   ❶

Her religion is <u>really</u> **out there**. They believe that God
lives in a UFO.

see also:  BATTY, BONKERS, KOOKY, LOONEY, NUTS, OFF THE
WALL, OUT IN LEFT FIELD, OUT TO LUNCH, SCREWY,
WAY-OUT, WHACKED-OUT, WHACKO, WHACKY

**out to lunch** [aut tə lʌntʃ] *adj* not in touch with   ❶
the real world, crazy

That guy's <u>totally</u> **out to lunch**. He thinks he can read
other people's minds.

see also:  BATTY, BONKERS, KOOKY, LOONEY, NUTS, OFF THE
WALL, OUT IN LEFT FIELD, OUT THERE,  SCREWY,
WAY-OUT, WHACKED-OUT, WHACKO, WHACKY

# P

**packrat** [pǽkræt] *n* someone who saves unneeded   ❶
items

My <u>dad's</u> a <u>real</u> **packrat**. He keeps all of his old
magazines and newspapers.

**pad** [pæd] *n* apartment, living quarters ❶

He has a beautiful **pad**.

**pain (in the neck)** [pein in ðə nék] *n* annoyance ❶

Will you please stop playing that drum in the house? You're being a <u>real</u> **pain** today.

Having to walk the dog every day is a **pain in the neck**.

see also: HEADACHE, PAIN

**party** [párdi:] *v* to celebrate, dance, and drink ❸

We **partied** <u>like crazy</u> last night. Too bad you couldn't come.

see also: HAVE A BALL

**party animal** [pɑrdi: ǽniməl] *n* someone who likes ❸ to party

That guy's a **party animal**. He lives for music, dancing, women, and beer.

**party pooper** [párdi: pùːpər] *n* someone who refuses ❶ to join in the fun

<u>C'mon</u> Bob, don't be a **party pooper**. If you leave now we won't have enough people to play cards all night.

see also: KILLJOY, FUDDY-DUDDY, STICK-IN-THE-MUD, WET BLANKET

**payback time** [péibæk taim] *n* time to repay a debt, ❶ a time to take revenge

A: No, don't shoot!

B: You murdered my brother. Now it's **payback time**, <u>asshole</u>.

**pay off** [pei ɔ́ːf] *v* to bribe ❶

The Mafia was **paying off** crooked <u>cops</u>.

**pay one's dues** [pei wʌnz dúːz] *v* to earn something ❶
by hard work or suffering

You <u>gotta</u> **pay your dues** if you want to be a sumo
wrestler. You <u>gotta</u> cook and clean for the older players
for years.

**pea-brain** [píː brein] *n* a stupid person, dimwit ❶

She says her new boyfriend's a **pea-brain**, but he sure is
cute.

see also: AIRHEAD, BIRDBRAIN, BLOCKHEAD, BONEHEAD, BOZO,
CRETIN, DIMWIT, DINGBAT, DITZ, DODO, DOPE,
DUMBELL, DUMMY, GOOF, GOOFBALL, KNUCKLEHEAD,
LAMEBRAIN, MEATHEAD, NINCOMPOOP, NUMBSKULL,
RETARD, SCATTERBRAIN, SPACE CADET, TWIT

**peanuts** [píːnʌtz] *n* a small amount ❶

You're only getting five dollars an hour? That's
**peanuts**!

see also: DICK, DIDDLY, JACK SHIT, SQUAT, ZILCH, ZIP

**pecker** [pékər] *n* penis ❹

He says he's got a long **pecker**.

see also: COCK, DICK, JOHNSON, PRICK, WEENIE, WILLY

**pee** [piː] *n* urine ❸

Don't touch that yellow snow! There's **pee** on it.

see also: PISS

**pee** [piː] *v* to urinate ❸

<u>Man</u>, I shouldn't have drunk so many beers. I <u>really</u>
have to **pee**.

see also: PISS

**peeping Tom** [píːpiŋ tám] *n* a voyeur ❶

John is a **peeping Tom**. He uses binoculars to watch
girls undress.

169

**peewee** [píːwiː] *n* a small person, sometimes a term ❷
of address for a small person

You're a **peewee**. You'll never make it as a football
player!

Hey **Peewee**, you want to try fishing?

> see also: PIP-SQUEAK, SHRIMP, SQUIRT, TWIRP

**pencil-neck geek** [pensil nek gíːk] *n* a physically ❸
weak and socially awkward person

The only guys who seem to find me attractive are
**pencil-neck geeks**.

> see also: GEEK, LOSER, NERD, WIMP, WUSS

**pep** [pep] *n* vitality, energy ❶

I can't stand people who are always complaining. I like
people with a lot of **pep**.

> see also: GET UP AND GO, PIZZAZZ, SPARK, SPUNK

**perks** [pərks] *n* benefits ❶

His salary isn't real high, but he gets a lot of **perks** like
a company car and health insurance.

**pesky** [péskiː] *adj* annoying, bothersome ❶

Peter's really **pesky**. He's always asking me to do his
homework for him.

> see also: IN ONE'S FACE, PESTY, PUSHY

**pester** [péstər] *v* to annoy, bother ❶

Stop **pestering** me! I'll clean the catbox later.

> see also: BUG, HASSLE

**pesty** [pésti:] *adj* annoying ❶

A: I want to stop for ice cream Daddy!

B: <u>OK</u>, <u>OK</u>, we will. Now, stop being so **pesty**.

see also:  IN ONE'S FACE, PESKY, PUSHY

**pet** [pet] *v* to touch sexually ❹

She let him **pet** her, but said she would not go all the way 'till they got married.

see also:  NECK, FOOL AROUND, MAKE OUT, SCREW AROUND

**peter out** [pi:tər áut] *v* to slowly decline or disappear ❶

He was <u>real</u> popular for about a year, but then his fame **petered out**.

see also:  FIZZLE OUT

**"phew!"** [fju:] *inter* expression of relief, fatigue or ❶
surprise

**Phew**! What a relief. I was worried this test would show I had AIDS.

**Phew**! It's hot out here!

see also:  WHEW

**phone** [foun] *n* [from *telephone*] a telephone set ❶

Can I use your **phone**?

**phone** [foun] *v* [from *telephone*] to contact someone ❶
by telephone

**Phone** me around five tomorrow and I'll be home.

**phony** [fóuni:] *adj* insincere, imitation ❶

I hate **phony** people. If you have money or are famous they want to be your friend, otherwise they ignore you.

This isn't a real fur coat. It's made of **phony** fur.

He thought he bought a real diamond, but it turned out to be **phony**.

see also:  BOGUS, FAKE

**phony** [fóuniː] *n* a person or thing that is not genuine ❶

He acts like he knows everything, but he's a **phony**. He doesn't <u>really</u> know anything.

**pick on** [pík ɔn] *v* to tease or torment ❶

All the other reindeer **picked on** Rudolph.

see also:  TAKE IT OUT ON

**pick-up line** [pík ʌp lain] *n* glib or persuasive words ❶ used to attract a potential lover

He uses the same **pick-up line** every time.

see also:  COME-ON

**picky** [píkiː] *adj* difficult to please, finicky ❶

Cats are <u>real</u> **picky** about what they eat.

He proposed to her last week but she refused. I know he's not perfect, but she shouldn't be so **picky**. She's already thirty years old and not so perfect either.

see also:  FUSSY

**piece of cake** [píːs ʌv keik] *n* something easily ❶ accomplished

A: Did you pass the test?

B: Yeah, it was a **piece of cake**.

see also:  BREEZE, CINCH, SNAP

**piece of shit** [piːs ʌv ʃit] *n* junk, something ❹ undesirable

I hate my car. It's a **piece of shit**.

You paid twenty dollars for this **piece of shit**? It's not even worth five.

I like her, but her brother treats me like I'm a **piece of shit**.

see also:   PILE OF JUNK

**pig** [pig] *n* disrespectful term for the police ❺

Here come the **pigs**. You'd better run.

see also:   COP, FUZZ

**pig** [pig] *n* a sloppy or obnoxious person ❹

<u>God</u>, Peter, why do you have to be such a **pig**? Can't you clean up after yourself?

Why do you let him bother you? He's nothing but a fat **pig**.

see also:   HOG, SLOB

**pig out** [pig áut] *v* to eat ravenously, gorge oneself ❶

Every Thanksgiving Americans **pig out** on turkey and pumpkin pie.

see also:   CHOW DOWN, PORK OUT

**pile of junk** [pail ʌv dʒʌ́ŋk] *n* something of poor quality ❶

My car is a **pile of junk**. You want it?

see also:   PIECE OF SHIT

**pile of shit** [pail ʌv ʃit] *n* junk, anything worthless ❹

This house is falling apart. It looks like a **pile of shit**.

I've got a **pile of shit** to do today.

**pimp** [pimp] *n* a man who secures customers for prostitutes ❶

That **pimp** has got five <u>hookers</u> working for him.

**pinkie** [pínkiː] *n* the little finger ❶

She was wearing a ring on her **pinkie**.

**pipe dream** [páip driːm] *n* an impossible dream, ❶
a vain hope

He's forty-five and still thinks he can become a
television star. It's just another one of his **pipe dreams**.

**pip-squeak** [píp skwiːk] *n* a little person or thing ❷

My dog's a **pip-squeak**. She's even smaller than a
Chihuahua.

see also: PEEWEE, SQUIRT

**piss** [pis] *n* urine ❹

There's **piss** all over the stairwell.

see also: PEE

**piss** [pis] *v* to urinate ❹

In America, men don't **piss** in the street like they do in
Japan.

see also: PEE

**pissed (off)** [pist ɔːf] *adj* angry ❹

My girlfriend was really **pissed off** at me when I
showed up late for our date.

I was **pissed** at my Mom for a week after she burned a
hole in my favorite shirt with an iron.

see also: BENT OUT OF SHAPE, TICKED OFF

**pisser** [písər] *n* something that is very funny or a lot of ❹
fun

That ride was a **pisser**. Let's try the roller coaster next.

see also: BLAST, GAS, RIOT

**pisser** [písər] *n* a difficult task or situation ❹

Man, that math test was <u>really</u> a **pisser**.

**piss-poor** [pis puər] *adj* very poor, penniless ❹

We're so **piss-poor** we can't even afford to rent a movie.

see also: BROKE, FLAT BROKE

**pits (the)** [ðə pits] *n* a depressing situation ❸

Dorm life is **the pits**. I can't wait to get my own apartment.

see also: BUMMER, DOWNER, DRAG

**pizzazz** [pizǽz] *n* the quality of being exciting or attractive ❶

I want to get a car that has some **pizzazz**.

see also: GET UP AND GO, PEP, SPARK, SPUNK

**PJ's** [píː dʒeiz] *n* [from *pajamas*] nightclothes ❷

Mommy, can I wear my flannel **PJ's** tonight?

see also: JAMMIES

**plain lie** [plein lái] *n* an obvious falsehood ❶

The Chinese government said that nobody was killed at Tiananmen. That's just a **plain lie**.

see also: BULLSHIT, STORY

**plastered** [plǽstərd] *adj* drunk ❸

Let me drive, <u>OK</u>? You're too **plastered** to be behind the wheel.

see also: HAMMERED, SHITFACED, SLOSHED, SMASHED, WASTED

**play dirty** [plei dɜ́rdiː] *v* to cheat or break the rules  ❶

Hey, if you **play dirty**, I will too.

see also:  FIGHT DIRTY

**play hardball** [plei hárdbɔːl] *v* to play aggressively  ❶
and ruthlessly

We're going to **play hardball** with the insurance
company. We've already hired a lawyer.

**play it cool** [plei it kuːl] *v* to act cautiously or  ❶
shrewdly, to feign disinterest

We need to **play it cool** if we're going to invest in
high-risk stocks.

I hate the way that guy is always **playing it cool**, like
nothing matters to him.

**plop** [plɑp] *v* to fall or drop with the sound of  ❶
something falling into water

His <u>turd</u> **plopped** into the toilet.

**polish off** [pɑliʃ ɔ́ːf] *v* to finish or dispose of  ❶

I'm <u>gonna</u> **polish off** this ice cream before I go to bed.

**pooped** [puːpt] *adj* tired, fatigued  ❷

I'm **pooped**. I can't believe I actually climbed Mount
Fuji today.

see also:  BEAT, BLEARY-EYED, BURNED OUT, BUSHED, DEAD,
FRAZZLED, FRIED, OUT OF IT, WASTED, WIPED OUT,
ZONKED OUT

**poo/poop** [puː, puːp] *n* excrement  ❷

Oh yuck! There's dog **poo** in the garden.

<u>Gross</u>! Somebody forgot to flush their **poo** down the
toilet!

see also:  CRAP, DOO-DOO, DUMP, SHIT, TURD

**poo/poop** [puː, puːp] *v* to defecate ❷

Mommy, can you take me to the toilet? I have to **poo**.

see also:  CRAP, DUMP, SHIT

**pop** [pɑp] *n* [from *papa*] father, also as term of address ❶

I don't know the answer but I'll bet you your **pop** does.

see also:  DAD, DADDY, OLD MAN

**pop** [pɑp] *v* to open quickly with a sharp sound ❶

He **popped** the lid off the bottle.

**pop!** [pɑp] *n* a sharp explosive sound ❶

The champagne went "**pop**!" when he opened it.

**pork** [pɔrk] *v* to engage in sexual intercourse ❺

Man, that girl's hot. Wouldn't you just love to **pork** her?

see also:  BANG, FUCK, HUMP, MAKE LOVE

**porker** [pɔ́rkər] *n* an obese person ❹

When she married him he was cute, but now he's a real **porker**.

see also:  BLIMP, FATSO

**pork out** [pɔrk áut] *v* to eat ravenously, gorge oneself ❸

A: How was lunch?

B: It was great. We **porked out** for two hours.

see also:  CHOW DOWN, PIG OUT

**porky** [pɔ́rkiː] *adj* fat, chubby ❸

He should start exercising. He's starting to get a little **porky**.

see also:  BLIMP

**posh** [pɑʃ] *adj* luxurious, elegant ❶

We went to this <u>really</u> **posh** restaurant last week, and ate lobster with truffles.

see also:  GLITZY, RITZY, SNAZZY

**pot** [pɑt] *n* marijuana ❸

Where can I get some **pot** around here?

see also:  DOPE, GRASS, WEED

**pothead** [páthed] *n* a person who smokes pot ❸
regularly

He turned into a <u>real</u> **pothead** when he started hanging out with those druggie friends of his.

**pow!** [pau] *adv* with violent abruptness ❶

He hit him in the face, and **pow**! the <u>guy</u> fell down.

see also:  BAM, BOOM, KABOOM, WHAM

**prayer** [préijər] *n* a slight chance ❶

You don't have a **prayer** of winning the race. Why even bother?

**preppy** [prépiː] *adj* neat in appearance, partial to a ❶
conservative style of dress

There are a lot of **preppy** students at Princeton.

see also:  YUPPIE, WASPY

**pricey** [práisiː] *adj* expensive ❶

These gourmet supermarkets are <u>really</u> **pricey**.

see also:  STEEP

**prick** [prik] *n* penis ❺

He's claims he's got a huge **prick**.

see also:  COCK, DICK, JOHNSON, PECKER, WEENIE, WILLY

**prick** [prik] *n* a contemptible person ❺

I hate that **prick**. He's one hateful <u>motherfucker</u>.

see also: ASSHOLE, BASTARD, COCKSUCKER, CREEP, DICK,
DICKWEED, DIP, DIPSHIT, DOUCHE BAG, FUCK, FUCKER,
JERK, MOTHERFUCKER, SCHMUCK, SOB, SON OF A BITCH

**princess** [prínses] *n* a spoiled girl or woman ❶

All she thinks about is her image, her clothes, and
herself. She's a <u>real</u> **princess**.

see also: JAP

**protection money** [proutékʃən mʌniː]
*n* money extorted by gangs posing as a protective ❶
association

Hey <u>man</u>, if you don't pay us **protection money** like all
the other shop owners, your place might burn down <u>or
something</u>.

**psyched** [saikt] *adj* excited, energized ❸

I'm <u>really</u> **psyched** to go to Australia this summer.

see also: GUNG HO, KEEN, PUMPED

**psycho** [sáikou] *adj* crazy, dangerous ❸

When he's angry he acts **psycho**. I'm afraid he might
kill someone.

He turns into a **psycho** <u>asshole</u> when he's drunk.

see also: NUTS, WHACKO

**psycho** [sáikou] *n* a crazy and dangerous person ❸

That guy's a <u>total</u> **psycho**. I would stay away from him
if I were you.

see also: MAD DOG

**psych out** [saik áut] *v* to undermine the confidence of ❸
or intimidate a competitor

The army was trying to **psych out** the enemy by
playing loud music and shining bright lights on their
compound.

**puke** [pjuːk] *n* throw up, vomit ❸

Oh <u>gross</u>! There's **puke** on the sofa!

**puke** [pjuːk] *v* to throw up, to vomit ❸

Oh <u>great</u>. Somebody **puked** in the sink.

see also: BARF, BOOT, HEAVE, THROW UP

**pull** [pul] *n* influence, political power ❶

He has a lot of **pull** in Washington.

see also: CLOUT

**pull someone's leg** [pul sʌmwʌnz lég] *v* to tease ❶
or fool someone

A: I'm pregnant with your baby.

B: **You're pulling my leg**!

A: No, I'm not. I really am pregnant.

**pull (something) off** [pul ɔ́ːf] *v* to succeed against ❶
the odds

Rajiv said he was going to study at an American
university. His parents didn't think he would make it,
but he **pulled it off**.

**pumped/pumped up** [pʌmpt, pʌmpt ʌ́p] ❶
*adj* excited, enthusiastic

All the football players were <u>really</u> **pumped** after they
won the game.

see also: GUNG HO, PSYCHED

**punk** [pʌŋk] *n* a young hoodlum or gangster, a ❶
troublemaker

I'd like to know the identity of the **punk** who stole my
car.

**pusher** [púʃər] *n* someone who sells drugs, a drug ❶
dealer

He started out as a **pusher** ten years ago and now
controls the drug trade in all New York.

**pushover** [púʃouvər] *n* someone who is easily ❶
defeated

I can't believe he gave in so easily. What a **pushover**!

see also: JELLYFISH, WIMP, WUSS

**pushy** [puʃiː] *adj* aggressive, demanding, annoying ❶

Some **pushy** lady wanted a seat, so she cut in front of
everybody waiting for the train.

see also: IN ONE'S FACE, PESKY, PESTY

**pussy** [púsiː] *n* the vagina ❺

You can see her **pussy** when she sits down. Why do
you think she isn't wearing any panties?

see also: BEAVER, CUNT

**pussy-whipped** [púsiː wipt] *adj* said of a man ❺
dominated by a woman

George is **pussy-whipped** by his wife. He <u>ain't</u> got no
<u>balls</u>.

**put down** [put daun] *v* to insult ❶

I hate the way he's always **putting down** his girlfriend
in front of everybody.

181

**put-down** [pút daun] *n* an insult ❶

He said you were too nice to be a lawyer? That's not a **put-down**, it's a compliment.

**putz** [pʌts] *n* a stupid, foolish, or clumsy person (also ❶ means penis)

That **putz** at the parking garage scratched the paint on my new car.

see also: SCHMUCK

**putzy** [pʌtsi:] *adj* stupid, foolish, clumsy ❶

If you're serious about college, you're going to have to spend more time studying and less time with those **putzy** friends of yours.

# Q

**queazy** [kwí:zi:] *adj* nauseous ❶

I felt **queazy** when I saw all the blood on the slaughterhouse floor.

**queen** [kwi:n] *n* disparaging term for an effeminate ❹ male homosexual

His brother is a **queen**, but he hasn't told his parents yet.

see also: FAG, FAIRY, FLAMER, QUEER

**queer** [kwi:jər] *adj* gay, homosexual ❹

He's proud of being **queer**.

**quick** [kwik] *adj* intelligent, fast thinking ❶

He's not too **quick** but he's <u>really</u> nice.

see also: SAVVY, SHARP

**quick fix** [kwik fíks] *n* a solution to a problem that ❶
addresses symptoms but not underlying causes

We need a **quick fix** for the computer before
tomorrow's presentation.

**quickie** [kwíki:] *n* brief sexual encounter ❶

They went into the bedroom for a **quickie**.

**quit cold turkey** [kwit kould tə́rki:] *exp* to ❶
abruptly cease the use of anything addictive

When my brother stopped smoking, he **quit cold
turkey**.

# R

**racket** [rǽkit] *n* loud noise ❶

Cut out the **racket** will <u>ya</u>! I'm trying to get some sleep.

He lives next to a railroad crossing. I don't know how
he can stand the **racket**.

**racket** [rǽkit] *n* a fraudulent scheme or activity ❶

He made a lot of money in some sort of mahjong
**racket**.

see also:  SCAM

**rack up** [ræk ʌ́p] *v* to accumulate or score ❶

The Yankees **racked up** ten runs in the first inning.

**rad** [ræd] *adj* [from *radical*] extreme ❶

Whoa! <u>Check it out</u>, <u>man</u>! That car is **rad**!

see also:  AWESOME, BAD, BADASS, CRAZY-ASS, EXCELLENT,
INTENSE, OUT OF SIGHT, OUT OF THIS WORLD, SUPER,
TO DIE FOR, WILD

**rage/raging** [reidʒ, réidʒiŋ] *v* to celebrate or party  ❶
intensely

We **raged** last night until three in the morning.

They were still **raging** when I left.

see also: PARTY

**rag on/rank on** [ræg ɔn, ræŋk ɔn] *v* to criticize or  ❶
harass

His friends are always **ragging on** him for being so
conceited about his hair.

see also: BAWL SOMEONE OUT, CHEW SOMEONE OUT, COME
DOWN ON SOMEONE, JUMP ALL OVER, JUMP ON, LET
SOMEONE HAVE IT, TAKE IT OUT ON

**raise hell** [reiz hél] *v* to cause trouble  ❶

He's **raises hell** when he gets drunk.

see also: MAKE A STINK, START SHIT

**R and R/R n' R** [ar ən ár] *n* [from *rest and relaxation*]  ❶

I think I'm gonna go to the Caribbean for a week
of **R n' R**.

**rat** [ræt] *n* a bad person, one who betrays an associate  ❶

Who's the **rat** that informed on me?

see also: BACKSTABBER, FINK

**rat on** [ræt ɔn] *v* to betray, inform on  ❶

I hope your little brother doesn't **rat** on us or we'll be
kicked out of school.

see also: SNITCH, SQUEAL, TATTLE

**rat race (the)** [ðə rǽt reis] *n* fierce competition to ❶
maintain one's position in the workplace or society

I quit my job on Wall Street because I was fed up with
**the rat race**.

**"rats"** [ræts] *inter* expression of dismay or ❶
disappointment

**Rats**! I thought I was going to win that contest.

see also: DAG, DANG, DARN, DRAT, GEE, GOLLY, GOOD GRIEF,
GOSH, JEEZ, SHOOT

**raunchy** [rɔ́ːntʃiː] *adj* smutty, dirty ❶

Look how **raunchy** that girl is. She looks like a <u>hooker</u>.

His house is pretty **raunchy**. I don't think he ever
cleans up.

see also: DINGY, SKANKY, TRASHY

**raw deal** [rɔː díːl] *n* an unfair arrangement ❶

The professor failed you <u>cuz</u> you forgot to sign your
name on the test? <u>Man</u>, that's a **raw deal**.

see also: BUM DEAL

**rays** [reiz] *n* sunshine ❸

<u>Wow</u>, what a beautiful afternoon! I'm <u>gonna</u> go outside
and catch some **rays**.

**real/really** [riːl, ríːli] *int* truly, unquestionably, ❸
authentic

His sister's **really** <u>awesome</u>.

He's a **real** nice <u>guy</u>.

I like people who are **real**, <u>ya</u> know? I can't stand
<u>bullshit</u>.

You're not being **real** <u>man</u>. Tell me what you **really** feel.

see also:  FOR REAL

**real man** [ri:l mæn] *n* a masculine man ❶

The only men who like me are eighty-pound weaklings. I want a **real man**.

see also:  HUNK, STUD

**rear end** [riər énd] *n* buttocks ❶

She's got a big **rear end**. Except for that, she's pretty skinny.

see also:  ASS, BOTTOM, BUM, BUNS, BUTT, FANNY, HEINIE

**red hot** [red hát] *adj* extremely popular, glowing with ❶ heat

That band's music is **red hot** right now.

Don't touch the burner, it's **red hot**.

**rednecks** [redneks] *n* insulting term for ignorant or ❹ unsophisticated rural whites

The Ku Klux Klan is full of **rednecks**.

John is a bit of a **redneck**, but he's changed a lot since he moved to Berkeley.

see also:  WHITE TRASH

**red tape** [red téip] *n* bureaucratic difficulties or delays ❶

It's not easy to get a green card in America. There's a lot of **red tape** involved.

**ref** [ref] *n* [from *referee*] one who officiates a sporting ❶ event

I think the **ref** made a bad call. Let's look at the instant replay.

**reject** [ríːdʒekt] *n* a pathetic person, one who is unable ❶
to succeed

That guy is such a **reject**. He acts like he's God's gift to
women, and <u>really</u> he's just a <u>dweeb</u>.

see also:  LOSER, LOWLIFE

**retard** [ríːtɑrd] *n* [from *retarded*] mentally or ❹
emotionally handicapped, a stupid person

How could you drive your bike into a parked car? What
are you, a **retard**?

He laughs like a **retard**.

see also:  AIRHEAD, BIRDBRAIN, BLOCKHEAD, BONEHEAD, BOZO,
CRETIN, DIMWIT, DINGBAT, DITZ, DODO, DOPE,
DUMBELL, DUMMY, GOOF, GOOFBALL, KNUCKLEHEAD,
LAMEBRAIN, MEATHEAD, NINCOMPOOP, NUMBSKULL,
PEA-BRAIN, SCATTERBRAIN, SPACE CADET, TWIT

**retarded** [riːtárdəd] *adj* mentally handicapped, ❹
foolish or stupid

He looks **retarded**, but he's actually a genius.

You gave all your money to your guru? How could you
do such a **retarded** thing?

**"right on!"** [rait ɔ́n] *inter* "Great!"  "Absolutely!" ❶
"Right!"

A: Women should have all the same opportunities as
men.

B: **Right on!**

**rinky-dink** [ríŋkiː diŋk] *adj* small or insignificant ❶

A: That watch you bought for yourself today is kind of
**rinky-dink**.

B: Yeah, well, it only cost three <u>bucks</u>.

All I got for Christmas was this **rinky-dink** T-shirt.

see also:  MEASLY, MICKEY MOUSE

**riot** [ráijət] *n* a wildly amusing person or activity   ❶

Your brother's a **riot**. He's the funniest person I've ever met.

Thanks for the great party. It was a **riot**.

see also: BLAST, GAS, PISSER

**rip off** [rip ɔ́ːf] *v* to steal   ❶

He made a lot of money by **ripping off** old people. He sold them stocks for gold that he didn't own.

**rip-off** [ríp ɔːf] *n* an act of thievery   ❶

Hamburgers cost twenty dollars at this restaurant! That's a **rip-off**.

**ritzy** [rítziː] *adj* luxurious   ❶

Let's stay in a <u>really</u> **ritzy** hotel when we're in Hawaii. After all, it is our honeymoon.

see also: GLITZY, POSH, SNAZZY

**rotten** [rátən] *adj* mean, bad, sick   ❶

How could you tell my sister she's ugly. That was a <u>really</u> **rotten** thing to say.

I feel **rotten** today. I think I'm <u>gonna</u> call in sick. I <u>gotta</u> take the day off.

**rough it** [rʌf it] *v* to live without modern conveniences   ❶

I like being in the woods, but I don't like having to **rough it** too much.

**rough time** [rʌf taim] *n* a difficult time, unreasonable   ❶ criticism

She's had a **rough time** ever since her husband died.

You shouldn't give your friend such a **rough time** about forgetting your birthday. I'm sure it wasn't intentional.

**rowdy** [ráudi:] *adj* noisy, out of control ❶

All the guys were getting too **rowdy**, so we left.

**rubber** [rʌ́bər] *n* condom ❸

I'm out of **rubbers** and I'm staying at my girlfriend's place tonight. Do you think you could give me a couple?

**rubberneck** [rʌ́bərnek] *v* to slow down when driving ❶ to look at an accident

Traffic was really slow because of all the **rubbernecking**. Everyone wanted to see the accident.

**"rubbish!"** [rʌ́biʃ] *inter* "That's nonsense" ❶

A: You said you would buy me a pearl necklace.

B: **Rubbish**! I said I would think about it.

see also: BALONEY, BULLSHIT, CRAP, FULL OF IT, GARBAGE, JIVE, TRASH

**rub it in** [rʌb it ín] *v* to harp on, especially something ❶ bad

A: Hey Bill, I heard you didn't get into Stanford.

B: Do you have to **rub it in**?

**runaround (the)** [ðə rʌ́nəraund] *n* evasive or ❶ misleading treatment

He asked her to marry him, but she won't give him a straight answer. She's been giving him **the runaround**.

**run-down** [rʌn dáun] *adj* damaged, poorly ❶ maintained

We live in a **run-down** old apartment in Harlem.

see also: BEAT-UP, CHEWED UP

**run-of-the-mill** [rʌn əv ðə míl] *adj* ordinary, average ❶

He lives in one of those **run-of-the-mill** towns in the Midwest.

**runs (the)** [ðə rʌnz] *n* diarrhea ❶

<u>Dad</u>, I have to go to the bathroom again <u>cuz</u> I got **the runs**.

**rush** [rʌʃ] *n* a feeling of excitement ❶

Skiing down that slope <u>really</u> gave me a **rush**.

see also: BLAST, BUZZ, CHARGE

# S

**sack** [sæk] *n* bed ❶

I'm <u>gonna</u> hit the **sack**. I'm <u>totally</u> <u>wiped out</u>.

**sack** [sæk] *v* to dismiss or fire an employee ❶

He got **sacked** for stealing from other workers.

see also: GET THE AX, LAY OFF

**S and M** [es ən em] *n* [from *sadism and masochism*] ❶

She's <u>really</u> into **S and M**, but she draws the line at being humiliated in front of others.

**"save it"** [séiv it] *imp* "Tell me later" or "Refrain from arguing" ❸

A: I <u>gotta</u> talk with you. I've got something that's been bothering me.

B: **Save it**, <u>OK</u>? I'm busy right now.

**savvy** [sǽviː] *n* practical intelligence ❶

That boy's got a lot of **savvy** when it comes to cars. He can fix anything.

see also: STREET SMARTS

**savvy** [sǽviː] *adj* intelligent ❶

You can't get anything past him <u>man</u>, he's as **savvy** as it gets.

see also: QUICK

**"say what?"** [sei wʌt] *inter* "What did you say?" ❸
"Are you kidding?"

A: I've decided that I want to <u>break up</u> with you.

B: **Say what?** Are you kidding me? I love you <u>baby</u>!

**SBD** [es biː díː] *n* [from *silent but deadly*] foul ❸
smelling intestinal gas that was passed silently

I hate it when people lay an **SBD** in the elevator.

see also: FART

**scam** [skæm] *n* an illegal, immoral or dishonest ❶
activity

He went to jail for being involved in a **scam** where he would sell swampland in Florida to people who wanted retirement homes.

see also: RACKET

**scared shitless** [skɛərd ʃítlis] *adj* very frightened ❹

I was **scared shitless** when I saw the shark coming at me.

**scare the shit out of** [skɛər ðə ʃít aut əv] ❹
*v* to frighten

Don't ever jump out of the closet like that again! You **scared the shit out of** me!

**scare up** [skɛər ʌp] v to locate, to find    ❶

I tried to **scare up** some money, but couldn't find any.

**scatterbrain** [skǽdərbrein] n a giddy or disorganized    ❶
person

I'm such a **scatterbrain**. I forgot my keys again.

see also: AIRHEAD, BIRDBRAIN, BLOCKHEAD, BONEHEAD, BOZO,
CRETIN, DIMWIT, DINGBAT, DITZ, DODO, DOPE,
DUMBELL, DUMMY, GOOF, GOOFBALL, KNUCKLEHEAD,
LAMEBRAIN, MEATHEAD, NINCOMPOOP, NUMBSKULL,
PEA-BRAIN, RETARD, SPACE CADET, TWIT

**scene** [siːn] n a fight; an exhibition of emotion    ❶

She made a **scene** at the party and embarrassed <u>the hell</u>
out of her boyfriend.

see also: BAD SCENE, STINK, TO-DO

**schlep** [ʃlep] v to carry or drag    ❶

A: Hey, those are the wrong books!

B: You mean I **schlepped** all these books over here for
nothing?

**schmuck** [ʃmʌk] n a mean person, a jerk    ❹

That **schmuck** crashed into my parked car and then
tried to drive away.

see also: ASSHOLE, BASTARD, COCKSUCKER, CREEP, DICK,
DICKWEED, DIP, DIPSHIT, DOUCHE BAG, FUCK, FUCKER,
JERK, MOTHERFUCKER, PRICK, SOB, SON OF A BITCH

**schnozz** [ʃnɑz] n nose    ❶

He has a huge **schnozz** but it looks good on him.

see also: BEAK

**school of hard knocks** [skuːl əv hɑrd náːks] ❶
*exp* the practical hardships and disappointments of life

A: He got fired from his job because he kept showing up late.

B: Well, there's nothing like the **school of hard knocks** to teach you how to behave.

**schtick** [ʃtik] *n* a special trait or behavior ❶

A: Why does she always act so cute?

B: It's her **schtick**. It's her way of getting attention.

He likes to be talked about by the literary crowd in New York, so he says outrageous things at parties. That's just his **schtick**, I guess.

see also: ACT

**scope (out)** [skoup aut] *v* to inspect intently ❸

I hate the way those guys sit in the corner and **scope out** every girl who walks by.

see also: CHECK OUT, EYEBALL

**score** [skɔːr] *v* to reach a goal; succeed in having sex ❸

He went to his neighbor's party uninvited and **scored** some food for us.

Did you **score** with her last night? Excellent! You lucky dog.

**screw** [skruː] *v* to have sexual intercourse ❺

He claims he's **screwed** hundreds of women.

see also: BANG, FUCK, HUMP, LAY, MAKE LOVE, PORK

**screw** [skru:] v to injure or betray someone ❹

If he thinks he can benefit from it, Leon won't hesitate to **screw** his friends.

see also: DOUBLE-CROSS, FUCK OVER, STAB IN THE BACK

**screw around** [skru: əráund] v to tamper with ❸

Kids, don't **screw around** with my stereo equipment, <u>OK</u>?

see also: FOOL AROUND, MESS AROUND WITH

**screw around** [skru: əráund] v to have casual sex ❹
with

He was **screwing around** with his secretary.

see also: FOOL AROUND

**screwball** [skrú: bɔ:l] n a strange or eccentric person ❶

My uncle is a real **screwball**. He thinks he has ESP.

see also: BASKET CASE, FREAK, FRUITCAKE, KOOK, NUTCASE, ODDBALL, WEIRDO, WHACKO

**screwed** [skru:d] adj in serious trouble or difficulty ❹

Look at this traffic jam! Now we'll miss my sister's wedding <u>for sure</u>. We're <u>really</u> **screwed**.

see also: DEAD, DONE FOR, FUCKED

**screwed up** [skru:d ʌp] adj confused, bad ❹

These instructions don't make any sense. They're <u>really</u> **screwed up**.

see also: FUCKED UP, MESSED UP

**screw up** [skru: ʌp] v to make a mistake ❹

Don't **screw up** your wedding day. Make sure you know where the church is!

see also: FUCK UP, MESS UP

**screwy** [skrúːi] *adj* crazy, silly ❶

He has some <u>really</u> **screwy** ideas. For example, he thinks it shouldn't be against the law to walk around naked outside.

see also: BATTY, KOOKY, LOONEY, NUTS, OFF THE WALL, OUT THERE, WAY-OUT, WHACKED-OUT, WHACKO, WHACKY

**"screw you!"** [skruː júː] *imp* a pointed insult ❺ "Go to hell!"

Hey <u>man</u>, **screw you**, <u>OK</u>? I don't have to take that kind of <u>shit</u> from anyone, especially from a <u>punk</u> like you.

see also: DROP DEAD, FUCK YOU, GO FUCK YOURSELF, GET LOST, GO TO HELL, SHOVE IT,

**scrounge (around)** [skraundʒ əraund] *v* foraging ❶ to obtain something at no cost

I was **scrounging around** for some loose change so I could take the bus home.

**scruffy** [skrʌfiː] *adj* rough and unclean in appearance ❶

I think you should shave. You look pretty **scruffy**.

**scrumptious** [skrʌmpʃis] *adj* delicious ❶

<u>Mmm-mm!</u> This ice cream is **scrumptious**.

**scum** [skʌm] *n* a base or worthless person ❹

I hate racists. They are such **scum**.

see also: DIRTBAG, DIRTBALL, SCUMBAG, SLEAZE, SLEAZEBAG, SLIMEBUCKET

**scumbag** [skʌmbæg] *n* a worthless or disgusting ❺ person

I hate that **scumbag**. He's the biggest liar I have ever met.

see also: DIRTBAG, DIRTBALL, SCUM, SLEAZE, SLEAZEBAG, SLIMEBUCKET

**scuzzy** [skʌzi:] *adj* dirty or shabby ❸

My car's pretty **scuzzy**. I think it's about time to wash it.

see also: CRUDDY, DINGY, GRUNGY

**"see ya' (later)"** [sí: jə leitər] *inter* [from *I will see you* ❶ *later*] "Goodbye"

**See ya'**. I've <u>gotta</u> go.

see also: ADIOS, CIAO, I'M OUTTA HERE, LATER, TAKE IT EASY

**sell oneself** [sel wʌnself] *v* to emphasize one's best ❶
features

If you want a job, you're going to have to **sell yourself**. Tell the employer why they should hire you.

**sell oneself short** [sel wʌnself ʃɔrt] *v* to fail to give ❶
oneself credit

Why are you always **selling yourself short**? You should be proud of your accomplishments.

see also: SHORTCHANGE

**sell out** [sel aut] *v* to compromise one's core beliefs ❶

He said he wanted to be a novelist, but became a lawyer for the money. I <u>guess</u> if you **sell out** like that, you'll never be happy.

**serious** [sí:ri:jəs] *adj* extreme ❸

We did some **serious** skiing down that mountain.

see also: INTENSE, WILD

**seriously** [sí:ri:jəsli:] *adv* intensely ❸

We were listening to this **seriously** crazy rock music.

**serious shit** [sìriːjəs ʃít] *n* an intense or somber issue ❺
or event

There is going to be some **serious shit** around here
when the boss finds out that someone read his personal
mail.

**sex fiend** [séks fiːnd] *n* someone obsessed with sex ❸

Joe's a **sex fiend**. He watches <u>porno</u> videos every
chance he gets.

see also:  NYMPHO, SLUT

**shack up with** [ʃæk ʌp wiθ] *v* to live together ❸

He **shacked up with** some blonde a couple of years
ago.

**shades** [ʃeidz] *n* sunglasses ❸

He always wears **shades** <u>cuz</u> he thinks they make him
look <u>cool</u>.

**shape up** [ʃeip ʌp] *v* improve one's behavior ❶

You're <u>gonna</u> get fired if you don't **shape up.**

**sharp** [ʃɑrp] *adj* intelligent ❶

That kid's <u>real</u> **sharp**. He always gets an A in math.

see also:  QUICK, SAVVY

**sharp** [ʃɑrp] *adj* stylish, attractive ❶

<u>Wow</u>, Tom! Is that a new suit? You look <u>really</u> **sharp**.

**shit** [ʃít] *n* excrement ❹

<u>Gross</u>! There's **shit** in the toilet! You forgot to flush the
toilet again John!

see also:  CRAP, DOO-DOO, DUMP, POO, POOP, TURD

**shit** [ʃit] *n* nonsense ❹

He's always talking **shit** about how he will be famous someday.

see also: BALONEY, BULLSHIT, CRAP, GARBAGE, JIVE, RUBBISH, TRASH

**shit** [ʃit] *n* criticism ❹

My dad's giving me a lot of **shit** about not studying enough.

Look <u>honey</u>, I've had a long hard day. Will you please stop giving me **shit** about not ever talking to you. I'm <u>pooped</u>, that's all.

see also: CRAP, HASSLE

**"shit!"** [ʃit] *inter* expression of anger, surprise, frustration ❹

**Shit**! I burned myself on the stove!

**Shit**! I forgot to go to the dentist today.

see also: DAMN, FUCK

**shitfaced** [ʃítfeist] *adj* drunk ❹

Last night we stayed out all night and got <u>really</u> **shitfaced**. That's why we all have hangovers today.

see also: HAMMERED, PLASTERED, SLOSHED, SMASHED, WASTED

**"shit happens"** [ʃit hǽpinz] *exp* "Unfortunate things happen" ❹

A: Her father was killed by a bus last week.

B: Yeah, well, **shit happens**.

A: Have a little sympathy, will you?

**shithole** [ʃithoul] *n* a lousy area, a foul place ❹

I live in a <u>real</u> **shithole**. The rats are larger than my cat!

see also: DUMP

**shitlist** [ʃítlist] *n* a list of things or persons disliked ❹

He's been on her **shitlist** ever since they broke up.

**shitload** [ʃítloud] *n* a large amount, a large number ❹

I have a **shitload** of <u>stuff</u> to do today, so I can't come to your book signing.

   see also: BUNCH, TON

**shitty** [ʃídiː] *adj* bad, lousy ❹

I feel **shitty**. <u>Ya</u> got any aspirin?

I can't believe I acted so **shitty** last night. I <u>guess</u> I should apologize.

This is a **shitty** camera. Next time I'm not <u>gonna</u> buy a cheap one.

   see also: CRAPPY, CRUMMY, FOUL, LAME, LOUSY

**shook up/shaken up** [ʃuk ʌp, ʃeikən ʌp] *adj* ❸
emotionally upset

She was <u>really</u> **shaken up** by the assassination attempt against her husband.

**"shoot!"** [ʃuːt] *inter* expression of surprise, anger, ❶
frustration

**Shoot!** I left my baseball bat at school.

   see also: DAG, DANG, DARN, DRAT, GEE, GOLLY, GOOD GRIEF,
         GOSH, JEEZ, RATS

**shoot up** [ʃuːt ʌp] *v* to inject a drug intravenously ❹

They were **shooting** her **up** with drugs so she couldn't talk.

The junkies were **shooting up** heroin in the alley.

**shortchange** [ʃɔrt tʃéindʒ] *v* to cheat someone, to ❶
give less than the correct change

The taxi driver **shortchanged** me.

  see also:  CON, HAD

**shortchange** [ʃɔrt tʃéindʒ] *v* to not give fair credit ❶

You shouldn't **shortchange** yourself like that. You have
a lot to offer.

  see also:  SELL ONESELF SHORT

**shorty** [ʃɔ́rtiː] nickname for a person of small stature ❹

Hey **Shorty**, maybe basketball is not the sport for you.

  see also:  SHRIMP, SQUIRT

**shot** [ʃɑt] *adj* broken, damaged ❶

He drank for too many years. Now his liver is **shot**.

  see also:  KAPUT

**"shove it!"** [ʃʌv it] *imp* [from *shove it up your ass*] ❹
a coarse insult

A: Hey, I was going to take that parking spot!

B: **Shove it!** I was here first!

  see also:  BUG OFF, DROP DEAD, FUCK OFF, FUCK YOU, GET LOST,
              GO FUCK YOURSELF, GO TO HELL, SCREW YOU

**show biz** [ʃóu biz] *n* [from *show business*] movie and ❶
theater business

**Show biz** is not as glamorous as you think. There's a
lot of <u>backstabbing</u> and lying.

**show off** [ʃóu ɔf] *v* to flaunt one's strengths or abilities ❶

He's always **showing off** how fast he can drive his
motorcycle.

He **shows off** his muscles whenever a beautiful <u>girl</u> walks by.

**show-off** [ʃóu ɔf] *n* someone who flaunts their strengths or abilities  ❶

He's such a **show-off**. He drives his Ferrari around just to impress the ladies.

**shrimp** [ʃrimp] *n* a small person  ❶

My little brother is a **shrimp**, but he's tough.

   see also:  PEEWEE, SHORTY, SQUIRT

**shrimpy** [ʃrímpiː] *adj* small and short  ❶

She doesn't like **shrimpy** men.

   see also:  PUNY, WIMPY

**shrink** [ʃriŋk] *n* clinical psychiatrist or psychologist  ❶

I have to go and see my **shrink** on Thursday.

**shut-eye** [ʃʌt ai] *n* sleep  ❶

I'm <u>gonna</u> go get myself some **shut-eye**.

   see also:  Z'S

**"shut the fuck up!"** [ʃʌt ðə fʌk ʌp] *imp* "Stop talking!"  a very strong insult  ❺

**Shut the fuck up** you noisy <u>asshole</u>!

**"shut up!"** [ʃʌt ʌp] *imp* "Stop talking!"  a mild insult  ❸

**Shut up!** I'm tired of listening to you complain about everything.

**sick** [sik] *adj* demented, disgusting  ❶

He told **sick** jokes at the wedding reception and embarrassed everyone.

**Sick**! There's <u>puke</u> in my bed.

see also:  GROSS, TWISTED, WARPED

# sick and tired of (to be) [tuː biː sik ən táijərd əv] ❶
*adj* no longer tolerant

I'm **sick and tired** of the way she talks to you.

see also:  FED UP WITH, SICK OF

# sick as a dog [sik æs ə dɔ́ːg] *adj* very ill ❶

He's been **sick as a dog** for a week. I'm worried he's got malaria.

# sicko [síkou] *n* a demented person ❶

Who's the **sicko** who hung a dead rat in my locker?

see also:  PSYCHO

# sick of (to be) [tuː biː sík əv] *adj* to be tired of, no ❶
longer tolerant of

I'm **sick of** other kids making fun of me just because I'm Korean.

see also:  FED UP WITH, SICK AND TIRED OF

# silent treatment [sáilənt triːtmənt] *n* the act of ❶
ignoring someone by resorting to silence

My girlfriend was <u>really</u> <u>pissed off</u> at me because she thought I was cheating on her. She gave me the **silent treatment** for a week!

see also:  COLD SHOULDER

# sis [sis] *exp* [from *sister*] term of address ❶

Hey **Sis**, what's up?

**sissy** [sísi:] *n* someone who is timid or cowardly ❷

C'mon Jimmy, aren't ya gonna cut school with us? C'mon, don't be a **sissy**.

   see also: CHICKEN, FRAIDY CAT

**situation** [sitʃju:éiʃin] *n* a set of life circumstances; a ❶ problem

He's got himself a real good **situation**. Try not to mess it up for him, OK?

We have a **situation** down here. Call the police!

**size up** [saiz ʌp] *v* to evaluate ❶

She **sizes** people **up** by the clothes that they wear.

**skanky** [skǽŋki:] *adj* dirty, promiscuous ❹

I hate that bitch. Look at her. She's nothing but a **skanky** hooker wearing **skanky** clothes.

   see also: SLUTTY, TRASHY

**skinny dipping (to go)** [tu: gou skíni: dipiŋ] ❶ *v* to swim in the nude

We went **skinny dipping** in the lake and it felt great!

**slack** [slæk] *n* breathing room, space, leniency ❶

Cut me some **slack**, OK? I'm not feeling well.

Give the kid a little **slack**, will ya? You're being too hard on him.

   see also: BREAK

**slammer** [slǽmər] *n* jail ❶

They threw him in the **slammer** for twenty years on a counterfeiting charge.

**slaughter** [slɔ́ːtər[  v to defeat overwhelmingly  ❶

They **slaughtered** us forty to four.

see also: CLOBBER, CREAM, CRUSH, KICK ONE'S ASS, LICK,
MASSACRE

**sleaze/sleazebag** [sliːz, slíːzbæg]  n a morally base  ❶
or worthless person

Why are you always hanging out with that **sleaze**?

I wouldn't do business with him again. I think he's a
<u>total</u> **sleazebag**.

see also: DIRTBAG, DIRTBALL, SCUM, SCUMBAG, SLIMEBUCKET

**sleazy** [slíːziː]  adj immoral, perverted  ❶

Most politicians seem pretty **sleazy** to me.

see also: DIRTY, SNEAKY, TWO-FACED

**sleep around** [sliːp əraund]  v to have sex with  ❶
many different partners

Her boyfriend was **sleeping around** on her for two
years before she found out about it.

see also: CHEAT, FOOL AROUND, TWO-TIME

**slick** [slik]  adj attractive, fashionable, shrewd  ❶

Hey <u>man</u>, that's a pretty **slick** automobile you've got
yourself there.

Who's that **slick** <u>dude</u> with the cell phone?

That <u>guy</u> is not my type. He's too **slick**. I like a <u>guy</u>
who's more down-to-earth.

see also: COOL, SMOOTH

**slime bucket** [sláim bʌkət] *n* an immoral or ❹
contemptible person

My boss is such a **slime bucket**. He's always trying to
get me to sleep with him.

see also: DIRTBAG, DIRTBALL, SCUM, SCUMBAG, SLEAZE,
SLEAZEBAG

**slob** [slɑb] *n* a sloppy person ❶

Tommy's a <u>real</u> **slob**. There are soiled clothes all over
his bedroom.

see also: PIG

**sloshed** [slɑʃt] *adj* drunk ❶

We drank so much that we were completely **sloshed** by
midnight.

see also: HAMMERED, PLASTERED, SHITFACED, SMASHED, WASTED

**slowpoke** [slóupouk] *n* a person who lags behind ❷

Hurry up will <u>ya</u>! We're late. Why are you always such
a **slowpoke**?

**slurp** [slərp] *v* to drink noisily ❶

He was **slurping** his soup.

**slut** [slʌt] *n* a promiscuous woman ❹

That **slut** says she's slept with at least fifty <u>guys</u>.

see also: BIMBO, EASY RIDE, HUSSY, NYMPHO

**slutty** [slʌdi:] *adj* sexually promiscuous ❹

He likes **slutty** <u>girls</u>.

see also: SKANKY, TRASHY

**smackeroo** [smækɑrú:] *n* a kiss; the mouth ❶

She gave me a big **smackeroo** on the cheek.

She punched him right in the **smackeroo**.

**small fry** [smɔːl frai] *n* a person with little influence, ❶
power, or rank

Don't waste time with some **small fry**. I want you to
catch the <u>head honcho</u> behind this <u>scam</u>.

**small print** [smɔːl print] *n* concealed conditions or ❶
penalties

That <u>deal</u> sounds too good to be true. You'd better read
the **small print** that explains how they intend to <u>screw</u>
you over.

   see also: CATCH, DOWN SIDE

**small talk** [smɔːl tɔk] *n* idle conversation ❶

We just talked about the weather. **Small talk** is
sometimes better than discussing painful things.

**small-time** [smɔːl taim] *adj* minor, insignificant ❶

He's just a **small-time** crook, so he's not a suspect in
the bank robbery.

   see also: CRAPPY, MICKEY MOUSE, RINKY-DINK, TWO-BIT

**smart aleck** [smɑrt ælik] *n* a prankster, an ❶
annoyingly self-assured person

Every time I tell Donny to clean up his room he tells
me to do it myself if it bothers me so much. He's
turning into a real **smart aleck**.

   see also: SMART-ASS, SMARTY-PANTS, WISE-GUY

**smart-ass** [smɑrt æs] *n* someone who talks back or ❹
is fresh

He always imitates the teacher in class. He's a <u>real</u>
**smart-ass**.

   see also: SMART ALECK, SMARTY-PANTS, WISE-GUY

**smarty-pants** [smárdi: pænts] *n* an obnoxiously ❷
conceited and clever individual

The other kids don't like her <u>cuz</u> she always acts like
such a **smarty-pants**.

see also: KNOW-IT-ALL

**smashed** [smæʃt] *adj* drunk ❸

Everybody at the party was <u>totally</u> **smashed** on my
homemade punch.

see also: HAMMERED, PLASTERED, SHITFACED, SLOSHED,
WASTED

**smidgen** [smidʒən] *n* a small amount ❶

I don't think there is even a **smidgen** of truth in what
he says.

Can I have just a **smidgen** more cake?

**smithereens** [smiðərí:nz] *n* many small fragments ❶
or bits

He stepped on a mine and was blown into **smithereens**.

**smooch** [smu:tʃ] *v* to kiss ❶

They were **smooching** in the back of the car.

see also: MAKE OUT, NECK

**smooth** [smu:ð] *adj* sophisticated and calm, shrewd ❶
and clever

Miles Davis plays some <u>real</u> **smooth** jazz.

That <u>guy</u> is too **smooth**. I just don't trust him.

see also: COOL, SLICK

**snag** [snæg] *v* to secure something ❸

She **snagged** herself a good man.

see also: NAIL

**"snag!"** [snæg] *inter* "Ha ha, I tricked you!"  ❸

A: You tricked me!

B: **Snag**!

see also: GOTCHA

**snag** [snæg] *n* an unforeseen hitch or obstacle  ❶

Everything was going fine until we hit this **snag** in the negotiations.

**snafu** [snæfú:] *n* [from *situation normal, all fouled up*]  ❶
a confusion or muddle

Our sales meeting turned into a complete **snafu**. The wrong invitations were mailed to the attendees.

**snap** [snæp] *n* something easy and quick  ❶

This game is a **snap**.

see also: BREEZE, CINCH, PIECE OF CAKE

**snazzy** [snǽzi:] *adj* fancy, stylish, and fashionable  ❶

Let's go celebrate at a **snazzy** restaurant.

That's a **snazzy** suit you've got on there.

see also: GLITZY, POSH, RITZY

**sneak** [sni:k] *v* to carry on secretively or furtively  ❶

He's always **sneaking** cookies out of my cookie jar. He's such a <u>sneak</u>.

**sneak** [sni:k] *n* a secretive, cunning person  ❶

I can't believe I married a **sneak**! How dare you read my diary!

see also: FINK, RAT

**sneaky** [sníːkiː] *adj* secretive and cunning ❶

You'd better watch that **sneaky** secretary of yours. I caught her taping my phone conversations.

see also: TWO-FACED

**snitch** [snitʃ] *v* to inform on ❶

He **snitched** on his friend to the police about the vandalism.

see also: RAT ON, SQUEAL, STAB IN THE BACK, TATTLE

**snoop** [snuːp] *v* to inspect in a meddlesome manner ❶

I don't like how my aunt comes in and **snoops** around my room.

**snooty** [snúːdiː] *adj* snobby, arrogant ❶

He's **snooty** just because he's the boss' son.

see also: ATTITUDE, COCKY, HIGHFALUTIN', SNOTTY, STUCK UP, UPPITY

**snooze** [snuːz] *n* a nap ❶

I'm <u>really</u> tired. I think I'll take a little afternoon **snooze**.

see also: SHUT-EYE, Z'S

**snooze** [snuːz] *v* to sleep lightly ❶

He wanted to **snooze** for just fifteen minutes, but he slept for three hours.

see also: CATCH SOME Z'S, CONK OUT

**snot** [snɑt] *n* nasal mucus ❸

<u>Gross</u>! There's **snot** coming out of his nose.

see also: BOOGER

**snot** [snɑt] *n* an obnoxious person ❸

That kid's a <u>real</u> **snot**. Somebody ought to smack him for being so <u>fresh</u>.

see also: BRAT

**snotty** [snádi:] *adj* covered with mucus ❸

All the kids make fun of him because he always has a **snotty** nose.

**snotty** [snádi:] *adj* obnoxious, annoying ❸

A: Clean up your room Johnny.

B: If you think it's so dirty Mom why don't you clean it up yourself?

A: Don't get **snotty** with me. If you don't do it I'll tell your father.

Nobody likes her because she's the **snottiest** kid in the school.

see also: ATTITUDE, COCKY, HIGHFALUTIN', SNOOTY, STUCK UP, UPPITY

**snow job** [snou dʒɑb] *n* an effort to deceive, ❸ persuade, or overwhelm with insincere talk

He must have written this report off the top of his head. It's a complete **snow job**.

see also: BALONEY, BULLSHIT, CRAP, GARBAGE, JIVE, RUBBISH, TRASH

**snug** [snʌg] *adj* comfortable, close fitting ❶

My sweater is **snug** already, so if it shrinks in the wash it'll be too tight.

**SOB** [esoubí:] *n* [from *son of a bitch*] a despicable ❹
person

I hate that **SOB**.

> see also:  ASSHOLE, BASTARD, COCKSUCKER, CREEP, DICK,
> DICKWEED, DIP, DIPSHIT, DOUCHE BAG, FUCK, FUCKER,
> JERK, MOTHERFUCKER, PRICK, SCHMUCK, SON OF A
> BITCH

**sock it to one** [sɑkitú: wʌn] *v* to strike someone ❶
hard, penalize severely

The IRS <u>really</u> **socked it to me**. I have to pay over a
million in back taxes. I'll be paying the bill for the rest
of my life.

**something else** [sʌmθiŋ els] *adj* said of something ❶
that is extraordinary

That <u>girl</u> is **something else**. I can't believe how <u>hot</u> she is.

**son of a bitch** [sʌn ʌv ə bítʃ] *n* a despicable person ❹

My ex-boyfriend is a <u>real</u> **son of a bitch**. I had an
abortion, and it was his kid, but he said it was my
problem and refused to help me pay for it.

> see also:  ASSHOLE, BASTÁRD, COCKSUCKER, CREEP, DICK,
> DICKWEED, DIP, DIPSHIT, DOUCHE BAG, FUCK, FUCKER,
> JERK, MOTHERFUCKER, PRICK, SCHMUCK, SOB

**sorry (ass)** [sɔ́ri: æs] *adj* pathetic, weak, useless ❶ ❹

He's always coming up with these <u>real</u> **sorry** excuses.
It'd be better if he said nothing at all.

That is the most **sorry-ass** car I've ever seen. Does it
even run?

> see also:  CRAPPY, CRUMMY, LAME, LOUSY, SHITTY

**soul** [soul] *n* deep feeling, a big heart ❸

That <u>dude</u> has got a lot of **soul**. He can play the sax like
no one else.

> see also:  HEART

**sound off** [saund ɔːf] v to complain loudly  ❶

His wife is always **sounding off** about how little money he makes.

see also:  BITCH, CARRY ON, GO ON AND ON, GRIPE

**sourpuss** [sáurpus] n someone who never smiles  ❶

Why is he always such a **sourpuss**?

see also:  CRANK, GROUCH

**space** [speis] v to forget, lose contact with reality  ❸

I can't believe I **spaced** my dentist appointment.

Don't **space** where you put my keys or we'll have to call the landlord.

see also:  ZONE OUT

**space cadet** [spéis kədèt] n a forgetful, unaware  ❸
person

You forgot to bring your passport with you? You **space cadet**! Our plane leaves in an hour.

Look, Bill's wearing his pants inside-out. He's a total **space cadet**.

see also:  AIRHEAD, BIRDBRAIN, BLOCKHEAD, BONEHEAD, BOZO, CRETIN, DIMWIT, DINGBAT, DITZ, DODO, DOPE, DUMBELL, DUMMY, GOOF, GOOFBALL, KNUCKLEHEAD, LAMEBRAIN, MEATHEAD, NINCOMPOOP, NUMBSKULL, PEA-BRAIN, RETARD, SCATTERBRAIN, TWIT

**space out** [speis áut] v to forget, to daydream  ❸

I was **spacing out**, thinking about how I would become a famous writer someday.

Listen to me, I'm talking to you. Why do you always **space out** when I'm talking to you?

see also:  TUNE OUT, ZONE OUT

**spacy** [spéisiː] *adj* dazed or stupified ❸

She's so **spacy** that I can't believe she'd ever pass a driving test.

see also: DITZY

**spark** [spɑrk] *n* positive energy ❶

She has a lot of **spark**, so we'd like her to be head cheerleader.

see also: GET UP AND GO, PEP, PIZZAZZ, SPUNK

**spastic** [spǽstik] *adj* physically uncoordinated ❶

I'm <u>really</u> **spastic.** I can't even catch a basketball.

see also: GOOFY, KLUTZY

**spaz** [spæz] *n* [from *spastic*] a clumsy or awkward ❸ person

He throws the ball like a **spaz**.

You **spaz**! You keep stepping on my feet.

see also: KLUTZ

**spiel** [ʃpiːl] *n* extravagant talk ❶

He was giving me his **spiel** about how he used to be handsome when he was young.

see also: ACT

**spiffed up** [spift ʌp] *adj* cleaned up, fancily dressed ❶

We got all **spiffed up** and went to New York for a fancy dinner.

see also: DECKED OUT, SPIFFY

**spiffy** [spífiː] *adj* neat, fine looking ❶

<u>Wow</u>, I've never seen you looking so **spiffy** before. You must have gotten a facial and a manicure today.

see also:   DECKED OUT, SPIFFED UP

**spitting image** [spitiŋ ímidʒ] *n* a replica ❶

Your son is your **spitting image**. I can hardly tell you two apart.

**split** [split] *v* to leave quickly ❸

All the crooks **split** when they heard the police sirens.

I <u>gotta</u> **split**. I'll see <u>ya</u> later.

see also:   BOOGIE, BOOK, CLEAR OUT, HAUL ASS, HIGHTAIL IT, HUSTLE, VAMOOSE

**split** [split] *v* to share ❶

Let's **split** the bill.

We **split** the cost of the hotel room <u>fifty-fifty</u>.

see also:   DIVVY

**split up** [split ʌp] *v* to separate ❶

We **split up** over a year ago.

see also:   BREAK UP

**spooky** [spúːkiː] *adj* scary ❶

It's <u>really</u> **spooky** in this cave. Let's get out of here.

see also:   CREEPY

**spring chicken** [spriŋ tʃíkin] *n* a young person ❶

You're not a **spring chicken** anymore. Maybe you should marry him even though he's not perfect.

**spunk** [spʌŋk] *n* fun and positive energy ❶

She has a lot of **spunk**. She loves to dance and jump around all the time.

see also:  GET UP AND GO, PEP, PIZZAZZ, SPARK

**square** [skwɛər] *n* person who is unfashionable or out ❶ of style

My dad is a <u>total</u> **square**. All he does is read books.

see also:  DWEEB. GEEK, NERD

**square** [skwɛər] *adj* unfashionable, unstylish

Our bass player is the **squarest** guy I know. He wears clothes that were in style twenty years ago.

**squat** [skwɑt] *n* the least amount, nothing ❸

He was a <u>shitty</u> teacher. I didn't learn **squat** from him.

see also:  DICK, DIDDLY, JACK SHIT, PEANUTS, ZILCH, ZIP

**squeal** [skwi:l] *v* to inform on ❶

Whoever **squealed** to the police is <u>gonna</u> pay.

see also:  RAT ON, SNITCH, TATTLE

**squirt** [skwərt] *n* a weak or small person ❶

Listen you **squirt**, if you don't pay me back, I'm <u>gonna</u> break your arms.

see also:  PIP-SQUEAK, SHORTY, SHRIMP

**squishy/squooshy** [skwíʃiː, skwúːʃiː] *adj* wet ❷ and/or soft

I touched a jellyfish. It was <u>really</u> **squishy**.

His foot felt all **squooshy** after he broke it.

**stab in the back** [stǽb in ðə bǽk] *v* to betray ❶

I trusted you to hold up your end of the bargain, but you **stabbed me in the back**.

see also: DOUBLE-CROSS

**stacked** [stǽkt] *adj* well endowed, big-breasted ❶

Whoa! That girl is really **stacked**.

see also: BUILT

**stand (for)** [stǽnd fɔr] *v* to tolerate ❶

It's not right to hit a woman. I won't **stand for** it.

I can't **stand** him. He's such an asshole.

see also: TAKE IT

**stand up to** [stǽnd ʌp tuː] *v* to confront ❶

He **stood up to** the Mafia, so they burned down his store.

**starry-eyed** [stári: aid] *adj* dazzled, dreamy thinking ❶

Ever since she met Tom she's been walking around **starry-eyed**. I guess she's in love.

**start shit** [stɑrt ʃít] *v* to cause trouble ❹

Everything was peaceful. Why do you always gotta **start shit**? You're a real troublemaker!

see also: MAKE A STINK, RAISE HELL

**starving** [stárviŋ] *adj* extremely hungry ❶

Let's stop here and eat. I'm **starving**.

**stash** [stǽʃ] *n* a hidden amount of drugs or money ❶

He was lucky that the cops didn't find the **stash** of coke he had hidden behind the toilet.

**steady** [stédi:] *adj* long-term or serious, exclusively ❶
dating

I don't have a **steady** girlfriend but sometimes I go on
dates <u>and stuff</u>.

They've been going **steady** for more than a year now.

**steal** [sti:l] *n* a bargain ❶

I bought this house for half of what it was <u>really</u> worth.
It was a **steal**.

   see also: DIRT CHEAP

**steep** [sti:p] *adj* expensive ❶

That's pretty **steep** rent. I can't afford even half that
much.

   see also: PRICEY

**"step on it!"** [stép ɔn it] *imp* "Hurry up!" ❶

<u>C'mon</u> kids, **step on it!** We have to leave in five
minutes or else we'll miss our plane.

   see also: BOOGIE, HAUL ASS, HIGHTAIL IT, HUSTLE, VAMOOSE

**stick around** [stik əráund] *v* to remain ❶

**Stick around** for twenty minutes, <u>OK</u>? I don't want us
to be seen leaving together.

**stick-in-the-mud** [stík in ðə mʌd] *n* a person ❶
who is old-fashioned or unprogressive

Bob never wants to have fun. He's such a
**stick-in-the-mud**.

   see also: FUDDY-DUDDY, KILLJOY, PARTY POOPER, WET BLANKET

**stick it out** [stik it áut] v to endure something ❶

She's not happy with her marriage, but wants to **stick it out** for the kids.

see also: HANG IN THERE

**sticks** [stiks] n a rural area ❶

I could never live in the **sticks**. I need the excitement of a city.

see also: BOONDOCKS

**stick-up** [stíkʌp] n a robbery ❶

There was a **stick-up** at the bank yesterday.

see also: HOLDUP

**stick up** [stik ʌp] v to rob ❶

He tried to **stick up** the bank, but got locked in the vault instead.

see also: HOLD UP

**stink** [stiŋk] n a loud complaint ❶

Why does he always have to make such a **stink** about visiting my parents?

see also: GRIPE, MAKE A STINK, SCENE

**stink** [stiŋk] adj bad, lousy ❶

I think our relationship **stinks**. I want out.

see also: SUCK

**stinker** [stíŋkər] n a disagreeable person ❶

He's a real **stinker** sometimes. He says things just to bother people.

see also: GROUCH, SOURPUSS

**stinking rich** [stiŋkiŋ ritʃ] *adj* very wealthy ❶

If I were **stinking rich**, I would buy a yacht and sail aroung the world.

see also: LOADED

**stoned** [stound] *adj* intoxicated with drugs or alcohol ❸

Everyone at the party was **stoned** out of their minds.

see also: HIGH, WASTED

**story** [stóriː] *n* misleading narrative, a lie ❶

I <u>wanna</u> know where you were last night, and don't give me **some** story about your car breaking down.

see also: LINE

**straight** [streit] *adj* heterosexual ❶

He's **straight**, but most of his friends are gay.

**straight** [streit] *adj* conservative, boring ❶

That <u>guy's</u> not my type. He's too **straight** for me. I like <u>guys</u> with <u>spunk</u>.

**straight** [streit] *adj* honest ❶

I want you to be **straight** with me, <u>OK</u>?

see also: GIVE IT TO ONE STRAIGHT, UP FRONT

**straight** [streit] *adj* no longer using drugs or alcohol ❶

I'm <u>gonna</u> turn my life around. I'm <u>gonna</u> go **straight** and get off this poison. <u>Coke</u> is killing me.

see also: CLEAN

**street smart** [striːt smɑrt] *adj* possessing skills ❶
necessary to survive in an urban environment

I worry about him living in New York. He's not very
**street smart**. He might get killed.

see also: SAVVY, STREET SMARTS

**street smarts** [striːt smɑrts] *n* urban survival skills ❶

To survive in New York, you got to have **street smarts**.

see also: SAVVY, STREET SMART

**streetwise** [striːtwaiz] *adj* resourceful in an urban ❶
environment

He's **streetwise**, but doesn't know how to read or write.

see also: SAVVY, STREET SMART, STREET SMARTS

**strong-arm** [strɔŋ ɑrm] *v* to use undue force ❶

The Mafia tried to **strong-arm** him into borrowing
money.

**strung out** [strʌŋ áut] *adj* intoxicated with or ❶
showing the effect of drug or alcohol addiction

Look at her. She's **strung out** on <u>coke</u> again. You can
tell by the look in her eyes.

**stuck up** [stʌk ʌ́p] *adj* arrogant, conceited ❶

I think all <u>good-looking</u> guys are **stuck up**.

see also: ATTITUDE, COCKY, HIGHFALUTIN', SNOOTY, SNOTTY,
UPPITY

**stud** [stʌd] *n* a masculine man ❸

Her new boyfriend's a <u>real</u> **stud**. He's an ex-football
player and a lawyer.

see also: BABE, HUNK, REAL MAN

**stuff** [stʌf] *n* things, any material　❶

He took some **stuff** out of his bag and threw it away.

The closet is full of useless **stuff**.

He said some **stuff** in Latin that I didn't understand.

<u>God</u>, I hate this **stuff**. I can't do math. I give up.

**stuff** [stʌf] *v* to fill completely, to block　❶

He **stuffed** his face with food.

I'm **stuffed**. I can't eat any more.

His pockets were **stuffed** with money.

My nose is **stuffed** so I called in sick to work.

**"stuff (and)"** [ən stʌf] *exp* conversational filler　❸
meaning "and so on"

He said he loved me **and stuff** but I didn't believe him.

Yesterday I went to town and did some errands **and stuff**.

**stuffy** [stʌ́fiː] *adj* hot or humid, blocked　❶

It's <u>really</u> **stuffy** in here. Could you open the window please?

I have a **stuffy** nose and a sore throat.

**stuffy** [stʌ́fiː] *adj* stodgy, dull, boring　❶

She's so **stuffy**. I wish she could learn to enjoy life more.

　　see also: SNOOTY, UPTIGHT

**style** [stail] *n* an elegant or fashionable manner　❶

He has a lot of **style**. His clothes and his women are always beautiful.

　　see also: CLASS

221

**stylin'** [stailin] *adj* [from *stylish*] elegant or fashionable ❸

<u>Wow</u>, this car is **stylin'**.

**suck** [sʌk] *v* to be dreadful, objectionable ❹

Jimmy, you **suck**! You're the worst player on the team!

This job **sucks**! My boss is a <u>real</u> <u>prick</u>!

see also: STINK

**sucker** [sʌkər] *n* someone who is easily deceived or ❶
used

He sold the dying horse to some **sucker**. He told the
<u>guy</u> it was just resting.

see also: CHUMP

**suck up to** [sʌk ʌp tu:] *v* to curry favor ❸

I hate the way he is always **sucking up to** the teachers.

see also: BROWNNOSE, KISS ASS

**super/superduper** [su:pər, su:pərdú:pər] *adj* great ❸

I think your new boyfriend is **super**.

see also: AWESOME, BAD, BADASS, CRAZY-ASS, EXCELLENT,
INTENSE, OUT OF SIGHT, OUT OF THIS WORLD, RAD, TO
DIE FOR, WILD

**sure** [ʃuər] *adv* definitely ❶

She **sure** is <u>good-looking</u>.

**sure thing** [ʃuər θíŋ] *n* a certainty ❶

We haven't signed a contract yet, but the deal looks like
a **sure thing**.

**sweetie** [swíːdiː] *n* dear, darling, also a term of address ❶

**Sweetie**, can you bring me my toothbrush?

see also: BABY, HONEY, LOVEY

**sweet talk** [swiːt tɔːk] *v* to flatter, cajole ❶

It's funny how your brother can always **sweet talk** his way out of any bad situation.

Remember, men may **sweet talk** you, but they just want to <u>screw</u> you.

see also: BULLSHIT, CON

**sweet tooth** [swiːt tuːθ] *n* a desire for sweets ❶

I think I have so many cavities <u>cuz</u> I have such a **sweet tooth**.

**system (the)** [ðə sistəm] *n* the system of government and industry ❶

He hates **the system**. He thinks the government is spying on him.

# T

**tacky** [tǽkiː] *adj* in poor taste ❶

I can't believe she would wear a vinyl skirt to church. How **tacky**!

see also: CHEEZY, TRASHY

**"ta da!"** [tədɑ́] *inter* "Announcing!" "Surprise!" ❶

**Ta-da!** Here is your new suit! How do you like it?

**take a dump** [teik ə dʌ́mp] v to defecate    ❹

I have to **take a dump**.

   see also: CRAP, POO, SHIT

**take care of business** [teik kɛər əv bíznəs]    ❶
v to assume responsibility for one's affairs

Hey, stop the <u>bullshit</u>. We're not here to <u>mess around</u>.
We're here to **take care of business**.

**take five** [teik fáiv] v take a five minute break    ❶

<u>OK</u> everybody, **take five** and we'll try the dance again
when you come back.

**take it** [teik it] v tolerate, withstand    ❶

I can't **take it** anymore. I'm going to quit this awful job.

   see also: STAND

**"take it easy"** [teik it íːziː] inter "Goodbye"    ❶

**Take it easy** <u>man</u>, I'll see you later.

   see also: ADIOS, CIAO, I'M OUTTA HERE, LATER, SEE YA

**take it easy** [teik it íːziː] v relax    ❶

We were hanging out at the pool and **taking it easy**
when suddenly it started to rain.

   see also: CHILL, HANG, HANG OUT

**take it out on** [teik it áut ɔn] v to vent one's    ❶
frustrations on someone

Don't **take it out on** the kids just because your boss
yelled at you.

   see also: BAWL SOMEONE OUT, CHEW SOMEONE OUT, COME
           DOWN ON SOMEONE, JUMP ALL OVER, JUMP ON, LET
           SOMEONE HAVE IT, RAG ON

**take the cake** [teik ðə kéik] *v* to be an outstanding ❶
example, the best or worst

When it comes to being crazy, Charles Manson **takes
the cake**.

**talk back** [tɔːk bǽk] *v* to reply rudely or ❶
impertinently

A: Clean up your room Johnny, it's a real mess.

B: Oh, do it yourself.

A: Don't **talk back** to me like that! Do as I say or you'll
get a beating!

see also: LIP

**talk big** [tɔːk bíg] *v* to boast, to brag ❶

Don't believe everything he says. He always **talks big**,
but it's mostly <u>bullshit</u>.

see also: SHOW OFF

**talk (bull)shit** [tɔːk búlʃit] *v* to talk nonsense, to ❹
exaggerate

It's incredible the way he can **talk shit** for hours on end.

see also: BULLSHIT, TALK TRASH

**talk trash** [tɔːk trǽʃ] *v* to arrogantly boast or talk ❹

He's always **talking trash** about how famous he is. It's
complete nonsense.

The opposing players always **talk trash** to try and
break your concentration.

see also: TALK BULLSHIT, PSYCH OUT

**tattle/tattle-tale on** [tǽdəl, tǽdəlteil ɔn] ❷
*v* to inform on someone, to betray a friend

If you **tattle on** me I'm <u>gonna</u> beat you up.

see also: RAT ON, SNITCH, SQUEAL

**tearjerker** [tiərdʒərkər]

*n* an extravagantly pathetic story that causes one to cry ❶

That movie was a <u>real</u> **tearjerker**.

**teenybopper** [tíːniːbɑpər] *n* a teen-age girl ❶

He's almost forty, but his new girlfriend is just a
**teenybopper**.

**tell it like it is** [tel it laik it íz] *v* to speak the truth ❶

Don't try to sugarcoat the issue. Just **tell it like it is**.

see also:  GIVE IT TO ONE STRAIGHT, LAY IT ON ONE

**tell someone off** [tel sʌmwʌn ɔf] *v* to scold or ❶
rebuke someone

I **told her off** for lying to me.

**"that's tough"/"tough luck"** [ðæts tʌf, tʌf lʌk] ❶
*inter* "That's too bad, but I don't care"

A: I wanted to pay you the money I owe you, but I
   needed it to buy food.

B: **That's tough!** I want my money now!

see also:  TOUGH SHIT

**the half of it** [ðə hæf əf it] *n* the other, much longer ❶
part of a story

You think that sounds bad? Well, you <u>ain't</u> heard **the
half of it**.

**thing** [θiŋ] *n* a mental fixation or habit, a custom ❶

She's got this **thing** about being married to a fat man.

A: Why's everybody bowing?

B: Oh, it's a Japanese **thing**.

see also:  HANG-UP

**thingamajig** [θíŋəmədʒig] *n* a gadget, a complicated ❶
mechanical thing

Does anybody know how this **thingamajig** works?

see also: DOOHICKEY, GIZMO, WHATCHAMACALLIT

**this and that** [ðis ən ðæt] *n* various things, nothing ❶
specific

We talked about **this and that**.

I wasn't thinking about anything in particular, I was
just thinking about **this and that**.

**throw up** [θrou ʌp] *v* to vomit ❶

I was seasick and **threw up** every five minutes.

see also: BARF, BOOT, HEAVE, PUKE

**throw-up** [θróuʌp] *n* vomit ❶

There's **throw-up** all over the bathroom. Who's <u>gonna</u>
clean it up?

see also: BARF, HEAVE, PUKE

**ticked off** [tikt ɔf] *adj* mad, angry ❶

He was <u>really</u> **ticked off** after getting a parking ticket.

see also: BENT OUT OF SHAPE, PISSED OFF

**tight** [tait] *adj* emotionally close or intimate ❶

Those two guys are like brothers. They're incredibly
**tight**.

**tight spot** [tait spɑt] *n* a difficult situation ❶

Joe walked up to me after the wedding ceremony and
asked me to give a speech. All the guests were waiting,
so I couldn't refuse. He put me in a <u>really</u> **tight spot**.

see also: BIND, HOT WATER, IN DEEP SHIT, JAM, UP SHIT'S CREEK

**tightwad** [táitwɑd] *n* a stingy or miserly person ❶

Maybe your girlfriends wouldn't leave you if you weren't such a **tightwad**.

see also: CHEAPSKATE

**tippy-top** [típi:tɑp] *n* the very top, the highest point ❷

I can't reach all the way to the **tippy-top** of the Christmas tree.

**tip-top** [tiptɑp] *adj* superb, excellent ❶

I'm in **tip-top** shape now that I work out every day.

see also: SUPER

**tits** [tits] *n* female breasts ❺

Look at the **tits** on this chick! What a great calendar!

see also: BOOBS, KNOCKERS

**to boot** [tu: bu:t] *adv* additionally, besides ❶

He gave me a raise, and let me have an extra week of vacation, **to boot**.

**to die for** [tu: dái fɔr] *adj* desirable, delicious ❶

Oh my God! This soup is **to die for**.

see also: AWESOME, BAD, BADASS, CRAZY-ASS, EXCELLENT, INTENSE, OUT OF SIGHT, OUT OF THIS WORLD, RAD, SUPER, WILD

**to-do** [tu:dú:] *n* a major event ❶

There was a big **to-do** after her election because she was the first woman President.

see also: HOOPLA, HYPE, SCENE, STINK

**toe cheese** [tou tʃi:z] *n* foul smelling substance ❸
between one's unwashed toes

Man, I need to shower and wash off the **toe cheese**.

**together** [tuːgéðər] *adj* mentally organized, healthy, ❶
strong

She's one of the most **together** people I've ever met.

**"to hell with him/her/them/it"** [tuː hél wiθ him, ❹
hər, ðem, it] *inter* expression of anger, frustration or
disappointment

I'm tired of trying to make our marriage work. **To hell
with it!** I want a divorce!

    see also:  FUCK IT

**tomboy** [támbɔi] *n* a girl who acts in a boyish manner ❶

When she was a kid she was a **tomboy**. She always
played baseball with the boys.

**ton** [tʌn] *n* a lot ❸

She gave him a **ton** of love, but he rejected her.

There are **tons** of people in China.

I ate **tons** of ice cream, and now I feel sick.

    see also:  BUNCH, JILLION, SHITLOAD

**tool** [tuːl] *n* a socially awkward person who is ❸
ridiculed or abused

The **tools** hang out in the recreation room with all the
<u>dorks</u>.

    see also:  DORK, DWEEB, NERD

**too much** [tuː mʌtʃ] *adj* unbelievable, incredible, ❶
excessive

I can't believe how he <u>bosses</u> people around. It's <u>really</u>
**too much**. Who does he think he is?

**total** [tóutəl] *v* [from *total loss*] to destroy or ruin ❶
something

I lent him my car and he **totaled** it.

229

My car was **totaled** in the wreck.

They **totaled** the hotel room.

**total** [tóutəl] *adj* complete ❶

He's a **total** idiot. He doesn't even know you're supposed to stop at a red light.

**totally** [tóutəliː] *adj* completely, greatly ❸

He's **totally** in love with you. Do you feel the same way about him?

This is a **totally** delicious dinner.

see also: FLAT OUT

**touchy-feely** [tʌtʃiː fíːliː] *adj* excessively emotional, ❸ sensitive, or physical

I don't like it when people are **touchy-feely**. It makes me uncomfortable.

**"tough boogies!"** [tʌf búgiːz] *inter* "Too bad" ❷

A: I don't want to go and get the ball.

B: **Tough boogies!** It's your turn to get it.

see also: TOUGH SHIT

**"tough shit!"** [tʌf ʃít] *inter* "Too bad, but I don't care" ❹

A: Hey, I was going to park there!

B: Well, **tough shit**, cuz I got here first!

see also: THAT'S TOUGH

**traipse** [treips] *v* to wander nonchalantly ❶

I don't like the way she **traipses** around our house like she owns it.

**trap** [træp] *n* mouth                                                                                         ❶

I wish she would shut her **trap**.

see also: BIG MOUTH

**trash** [træʃ] *n* garbage, nonsense                                                                ❸

Don't believe a word he says. It's all **trash**.

see also: BALONEY, BULLSHIT, CRAP, FULL OF IT, GARBAGE, JIVE, RUBBISH

**trash** [træʃ] *v* to destroy or damage, make a mess                                    ❸

They <u>really</u> **trashed** his idea.

Those creeps <u>totally</u> **trashed** my house during the party.

see also: DIS, FLAME

**trashy (looking)** [trǽʃiː lukiŋ] *adj* low-class in                               ❸
appearance, ugly

He seems to like **trashy-looking** blondes.

All the houses in this neighborhood are pretty **trashy**.

see also: SKANKY

**trigger happy** [trígər hæpiː] *adj* aggressive,                              ❶
belligerent; irresponsible in the use of a gun

Be careful hiking in the woods during hunting season. Some of those hunters are **trigger happy**.

**trip** [trip] *n* the experience of being intoxicated with a     ❶
drug

He took acid and had a very scary **trip**.

**trip (out) on** [trip áut ɔn] *v* to have a drug-induced         ❸
experience

They were **tripping out** on mushrooms when his father walked in.

**trippy** [trípiː] *adj* relating to the use of psychedelic ❸
drugs; weird, bizarre

He has some pretty **trippy** ideas about the nature of
reality.

**trouble** [trʌbəl] *n* a dangerous person or situation ❶

You had better avoid that guy. He's **trouble**.

**tube** [tuːb] *n* television, TV ❶

The **tube** is always on in this house even when no one
is watching.

**tune out** [tuːn áut] *v* to ignore, become unresponsive ❶

When his wife nags him he just **tunes out** and does his
own thing.

> see also:  SPACE OUT, ZONE OUT

**turd** [tərd] *n* feces, excrement ❸

Somebody forgot to flush. There's a big **turd** in the
toilet.

> see also:  CRAP, DOO-DOO, DUMP, POO, POOP, SHIT

**turf** [tərf] *n* territory ❸

If I were you I wouldn't go down that street. It's the
other gang's **turf**.

**turkey** [tə́rkiː] *n* a foolish or inept person ❸

Check out the **turkey** who's trying to look cool over
there!

> see also:  LOSER, NERD, SUCKER

**turn in** [tərn ín] *v* to give over, hand in ❶

The crook **turned in** his partner to the cops so that
he'd get a lighter sentence.

**turn in** [tərn ín] *v* to retire to bed ❶

I'm <u>beat</u>. I'm <u>gonna</u> **turn in** for the night.

see also: HIT THE HAY

**turn off** [tərn ɔ́f] *v* to disgust, to cause to lose interest ❶

When I see someone smoke it <u>really</u> **turns** me **off**. I think smoking is revolting.

see also: GROSS SOMEONE OUT

**turnoff** [tə́rn ɔf] *n* a disgusting or revolting practice or thing ❶

Smoking is a real **turnoff**.

**turn on** [tərn ɔ́n] *v* to excite, especially sexually ❸

It <u>really</u> **turns** me **on** when you blow in my ear.

Tell me what you want me to do. I'll do whatever **turns** you **on**.

**turn-on** [tə́rn ɔn] *n* something exciting ❸

Long, lean legs are a real **turn-on**.

**twerp** [twərp] *n* a silly or contemptible person ❶

Her new boyfriend is a <u>real</u> **twerp**.

**twerpy** [twərpiː] *adj* silly, contemptible ❶

Why does she like that **twerpy** <u>guy</u>?

**twisted** [twistəd] *adj* emotionally or mentally disturbed ❶

He has a **twisted** way of looking at things. I don't think he should be put in charge of hiring.

see also: SICK, WARPED

**twit** [twit] *n* silly, annoying person ❶

I can't believe what a **twit** I am! I locked myself out of the house again.

see also: AIRHEAD, BIRDBRAIN, BLOCKHEAD, BONEHEAD, BOZO, CRETIN, DIMWIT, DINGBAT, DITZ, DODO, DOPE, DUMBELL, DUMMY, GOOF, GOOFBALL, KNUCKLEHEAD, LAMEBRAIN, MEATHEAD, NINCOMPOOP, NUMBSKULL, PEA-BRAIN, RETARD, SCATTERBRAIN, SPACE CADET

**two-bit** [tú: bit] *adj* bad, of low quality, shoddy ❶

I refuse to stay in some **two-bit** hotel. Let's get a place with a hot tub and sauna.

see also: CRAPPY, MICKEY MOUSE, RINKY-DINK, SMALL-TIME

**two bits/two cents** [tu: bits, tu: sents] *n* one's ❶
unsolicited opinion

No one asked you for your opinion. Why do you always have to put in your **two cents**?

**two-faced** [tú: feist] *adj* insincere, deceitful ❶

I don't trust that guy at all. I think he's completely **two-faced**.

That **two-faced** son of a bitch stabbed me in the back!

see also: SLEAZY, SNEAKY

**two-time** [tú: taim] *v* to cheat ❶

He **two-timed** his wife for years before she found out he was sleeping with his secretary!

see also: CHEAT, FOOL AROUND, SLEEP AROUND

**two-timing** [tú: taimiŋ] *adj* cheating ❶

I divorced him because he was a **two-timing** asshole.

**type** [taip] *n* the qualities of a person one is ❸
attracted to

He's cute, but he's not my **type**.

What's your **type**?

# U

**"uh"** [ə] *inter* used as a pause in conversation ❶

I, **uh**, went to the store and, **uh**, bought some milk.

see also: LIKE

**"uh-huh"** [ə hə́] *inter* yes ❶

A: Are you hungry?

B: **Uh-huh**. Let's go and get something to eat.

**"uh-uh"** [ə́ ə] *inter* No ❶

A: Are you hungry?

B: **Uh-uh**, I just ate.

see also: NAH, NOPE

**umpteen** [ʌmptíːn] *n* a very large number or amount ❶

I've told her **umpteen** times not to play her music so
loud at night, but she won't listen.

see also: JILLION, SHITLOAD, TON, ZILLION

**Uncle Sam** [ʌnkəl sǽm] *n* the US government ❶

**Uncle Sam** collects a lot of taxes from the working
man.

**uncool** [ʌnkúːl] *adj* bad, inconsiderate, selfish ❸

I think it was <u>really</u> **uncool** of you to yell at me in front of my friends.

**unreal** [ʌnríːl] *adj* unbelievable ❶

<u>Man</u>, this museum is **unreal**. I feel like I've gone back in time.

see also: MIND-BLOWING, MIND-BOGGLING

**up** [ʌp] *adv* positive, optimistic ❶

I feel **up** whenever it's sunny.

I was feeling <u>kinda</u> <u>down</u> yesterday, but today I'm feeling pretty **up**.

**up** [ʌp] *adj* awake, out of bed ❶

Is he **up** yet? We have to go.

**up-and-coming** [ʌp ən kʌ́miŋ] *adj* persons gaining ❶ popularity or influence

Who are the **up-and-coming** people in your field?

**up for grabs** [ʌp fər grǽbz] *adj* available to anyone ❶

My sister broke up with her boyfriend last month and now she's not goin' out with anyone. She's **up for grabs**. Why don't you give her a call?

America was **up for grabs** until five hundred years ago when the Europeans took it. If the Japanese had taken it, the whole world would speak Japanese now.

**up-front** [ʌp frʌnt] *adj* direct, sincere, frank ❶

I like it when people are **up-front** with me.

see also: STRAIGHT

**up in the air** [ʌp in ði: ɛər] *adj* not settled, unclear ❶

I still don't know if I'll be transferred to New York. The matter is still **up in the air**.

I don't know whether those two will stay married or get a divorce. It's still **up in the air**.

**uppity** [ʌ́pidiː] *adj* snobbish, arrogant ❶

People don't like her because she has a <u>real</u> **uppity** attitude.

see also: ATTITUDE, COCKY, HIGHFALUTIN', SNOOTY, SNOTTY, STUCK UP

**up shit creek (without a paddle)** [ʌp ʃit kriːk wiθaut ə pædəl] *adj* in serious trouble, in a bad situation ❹

When your <u>dad</u> finds out you wrecked his car you're <u>gonna</u> be **up shit creek**.

see also: BIND, HOT WATER, IN DEEP SHIT, JAM, TIGHT SPOT

**up side** [ʌp said] *n* a positive aspect ❶

There's an **up side** to your getting fired: you'll have a lot more free time.

see also: FLIP SIDE

**uptight** [ʌptáit] *adj* rigidly conventional, nervous, tense ❶

Our new manager is very **uptight** about enforcing the dress code. Everybody has to wear a shirt and tie.

He gets <u>really</u> **uptight** whenever I talk about my old boyfriends. I think he gets jealous.

see also: ANTSY, HIGH-STRUNG

**use** [juːz] *v* to exploit, to take advantage of ❶

He **used** her and then threw her away like she was a piece of garbage.

# V

**"vamoose!"** [vɑmúːs] *imp* [Spanish for *let's go*] to ❶
depart quickly

**Vamoose**! We're late already!

see also: BOOGIE, BOOK, CLEAR OUT, HAUL ASS, HIGHTAIL IT,
HUSTLE, SPLIT, STEP ON IT

**VD** [viːdíː] *n* [*abbr* of *Venereal Disease*] ❶

I always wear a condom so I won't get **VD**.

**vegetate/veg** [védʒəteit, vedʒ] *v* to lay around, do ❶
nothing

She sits around the house all day, **vegetating** in front of
the TV.

We just **veged** around the house all day.

see also: FART AROUND

**veggies** [védʒiːz] *n* [from *vegetable*] ❶

I try to eat **veggies** three times a day.

**"very funny!"** [vérɪ fʌ́niː] *inter* a sarcastic response ❶
to a comment made in jest

A: Train tickets are half-priced only for children.
You're an adult.

B: No, <u>really</u>, I'm only ten years old.

A: **Very funny**. You're at least twenty so I will have to
charge you the full fare.

see also: COME OFF IT, YEAH RIGHT

**vibes** [vaibz] *n* [from *vibrations*] an emotional ❸ atmosphere or feeling about a person or place

This place gives me bad **vibes**. I get the feeling that something very evil happened in this room.

I trust him even though I've only known him for ten minutes. I get good **vibes** from him.

**VIP** [vi:aipi:] *n* [from *Very Important Person*] ❶

Who is he, some sort of **VIP**?

The company is flying in all the **VIP's** for an important meeting.

see also: BIG SHOT, HEAD HONCHO, HEAVY

# W

**wad** [wɑd] *n* a clump, a bunch ❶

Watch out. There's a **wad** of gum on that chair.

He held up a fat **wad** of hundred dollar bills.

**wait up** [weit ʌp] *v* to stay up late waiting for ❶ someone

I **waited up** for him, but he never came home that night.

**"wait up!"** [weit ʌp] *imp* "Slow down!"

**Wait up!** I can't keep up with you.

**walk on cloud nine** [wɑk ɔn klaud náin] *exp* to be ❶ blissfully happy

She's been **walking on cloud nine** ever since they got engaged.

239

**walk out on** [wɑk áut ɔn] v to abandon a   ❶
responsibility or commitment

He **walked out on** his wife when he caught her
sleeping with his best friend.

You can't just **walk out on** this deal. We have a
contract.

  see also: BLOW OFF

**wanna** [wɑ́nɑ] v [from *want to*]

I **wanna** go to America.

If <u>ya</u> **wanna** speak English well, <u>ya</u> <u>gotta</u> speak it every
day.

**wanna-be** [wɑ́nəbiː] n [from *want to be*] a person   ❶
who wants to be someone else

Some foreigners in Japan are **wanna-bes**. They act
more Japanese than the Japanese do.

**want it** [wɑ́nt it] v to desire sex   ❹

Don't go out with that <u>guy</u>. He'll spend the whole
evening telling you how much he **wants it**.

**want out** [wɑnt áut] v desiring to be released from   ❶
responsibility or commitment

I don't care if I signed a contract. I still **want out**.

I **want out** of this marriage. You're too verbally
abusive.

**warmed-over** [wɔ́rmd ouvər] adj old, stale   ❶

I'm looking for writers with originality. Unfortunately,
your manuscript is just **warmed-over** Hemingway.

**warped** [wɔrpt] adj perverted, demented   ❸

He has a <u>real</u> **warped** sense of humor.

  see also: SICK, TWISTED

**WASP** [wɑsp] *n* [from *White Anglo-Saxon Protestant*] ❹
a dominant and privileged class of people

Nantucket is a favorite resort of New England **WASPs**.

**waspy** [wɑ́spiː] *adj* of or like a <u>WASP</u> ❹

She <u>really</u> cultivates that **waspy** look with her blonde hair and <u>preppy</u> clothes.

see also: PREPPY

**waste** [weist] *v* to kill, to destroy ❹

The soldiers all bragged that they would **waste** the enemy if they met them in the jungle.

see also: BUMP OFF, CRUSH, FRY, KICK BUTT, MASSACRE, SLAUGHTER

**wasted** [wéistəd] *adj* drunk ❸

Each of us drank ten beers and got completely **wasted**.

see also: HAMMERED, PLASTERED, SHITFACED, SLOSHED, SMASHED

**wasted** [wéistəd] *adj* tired, exhausted ❸

I've been up for two days, and feel pretty **wasted**.

see also: BEAT, BLEARY-EYED, BURNED OUT, BUSHED, DEAD, FRAZZLED, FRIED, OUT OF IT, POOPED, WIPED OUT, ZONKED OUT

**way-out** [wéi aut] *adj* strange, bizarre ❶

He's got a <u>really</u> **way-out** view of the world.

see also: FAR-OUT

**weed** [wiːd] *n* marijuana ❸

Let's go over to Pete's house and smoke some **weed**.

see also: DOPE, GRASS, POT

## weenie/wiener [wíːniː, wíːnər] n  penis

Put your **weenie** back in your pants!

see also:  COCK, DICK, JOHNSON, PECKER, PRICK, WILLY

## weenie [wíːniː] n  a weak or timid person  ❷

I don't like him <u>cuz</u> he's such a **weenie**. He's afraid of everything.

see also:  WIMP, WUSS

## wee-wee [wíː wiː] v  to urinate  ❷

Mama, I have to go **wee-wee**.

see also:  PEE

## weirdo [wíərdou] n a strange or odd person  ❶

He's a <u>real</u> **weirdo**. He meditates under a pyramid before breakfast every morning.

My older brother's a bit of a **weirdo**. He talks to himself and sometimes laughs for no apparent reason.

see also:  BASKET CASE, FREAK, FRUITCAKE, KOOK, NUTCASE, ODDBALL, SCREWBALL, WHACKO

## well-hung [wel hʌŋ] adj having a large penis  ❹

That <u>guy</u> may be ugly, but he sure is **well-hung**.

## wet blanket [wet blǽŋkət] n someone who ruins  ❶
the fun of others

I don't want him coming to our party. He's such a **wet blanket**. He'll ruin it for the rest of us.

see also:  FUDDY-DUDDY, KILLJOY, PARTY POOPER, STICK-IN-THE-MUD

## whack [wæk] v to hit or slap  ❶

She **whacked** him hard when he tried to kiss her.

see also:  BASH, BOP

**whacked-out** [wækt áut] *adj* crazy or weird

That <u>guy</u> is <u>really</u> **whacked-out**. He likes to punch the wall to make himself tougher.

> see also: BATTY, BONKERS, KOOKY, LOONEY, NUTS, OFF THE WALL, OUT IN LEFT FIELD, OUT THERE, OUT TO LUNCH, SCREWY, WAY-OUT, WHACKO, WHACKY

**whacko** [wǽkou] *n* a crazy or weird person

Why do you even want to hang out with a **whacko** like that?

I think people who believe in astrology are a bunch of **whackos**.

> see also: FREAK, FRUITCAKE, KOOK, NUTCASE, ODDBALL, SCREWBALL, WEIRDO

**whacko** [wǽkou] *adj* crazy, weird

I just don't trust that new friend of yours. He has a lot of **whacko** ideas.

> see also: BATTY, BONKERS, KOOKY, LOONEY, NUTS, OFF THE WALL, OUT IN LEFT FIELD, OUT THERE, OUT TO LUNCH, SCREWY, WAY-OUT, WHACKED-OUT, WHACKY

**whacky** [wǽki:] *adj* absurdly eccentric or irrational

That's the **whackiest** idea I ever heard.

> see also: BATTY, KOOKY, LOONEY, OFF THE WALL, OUT IN LEFT FIELD, OUT THERE, SCREWY, WAY-OUT, WHACKED-OUT, WHACKO

**wham** [wæm] *n* the loud sound of an impact

The door closed with a **wham**.

> see also: BAM, BANG, BOOM, CLUNK

**wham!** [wæm] *adv* with violent abruptness

The door went "**wham**" and <u>scared the shit out of</u> all of us.

> see also: BAM, BANG, BOOM, CLUNK

**"whassup?"** [wəsʌp] *exp* [from *What's up?*] "How are ❸ you?"

Hey <u>man</u>, **whassup**? How've you been?

    see also:  WHAT'S HAPPENING

**"whatcha"** [wə́tʃə] *exp* [from *What are you?*] ❶

**Whatcha** <u>gonna</u> do tomorrow?

**whatchamacallit** [wə́tʃəməkɔ:lit] *n* [from *what you* ❶ *may call it*] an object whose name one has forgotten

He gave her the **whatchamacallit**. The... <u>uh</u>, you know what I mean, right?

    see also:  DOOHICKEY, GIZMO, THINGAMAJIG

**"whatever"** [wətévər] *inter* [from *whatever you say*] ❸ "In any case"

A: It's you I love, <u>babe</u>. That other woman didn't mean anything to me.

B: <u>Yeah</u>, **whatever**. Just leave me alone, you <u>creep</u>.

    see also:  FORGET IT, FAT CHANCE, VERY FUNNY, YEAH RIGHT

**what it takes** [wʌt it téiks] *n* the necessary ❶ ingredients for success

If you just study more I'll bet you can pass the test. I know you've got **what it takes**.

**"what's happening?"** [wʌts hǽpəniŋ] *inter* general ❸ greeting inquiring about the state of one's life

Hey, **what's happening?** I haven't heard from you in <u>ages</u>.

    see also:  WHASSUP

**what's-his-face** [wʌ́tsiz feis] *n* a person whose name ❶
one has forgotten

A: Have you seen him around here?

B: Who do you mean?

A: You know, **what's-his-face**, the short ugly <u>guy</u>. I
can't remember his name.

**"what's the big idea?"** [wʌts ðə big aidí:ə] ❶
*exp* "What do you think you are doing?"

Hey you! Why are you reading my diary? **What's the
big idea?**

**"what's the deal?"** [wʌts ðə dí:l] *inter* "What is ❶
going on?", "Why are you acting like that?"

Hey, you're late. **What's the deal?** You were supposed
to meet me here forty minutes ago.

**"what's up?"** [wʌts ʌ́p] *inter* "How are you?", ❶
"Anything new?"

**What's up** Tom? How's your new job working out?

see also: WHASSUP, WHAT'S HAPPENING

**wheel and deal** [wi:l ən dí:l] *v* to do business ❶
briskly or shrewdly

He's always **wheeling and dealing**, trying to make
money any way he can.

see also: HUSTLE

**wheeler-dealer** [wí:lər dí:lər]
*n* a person who does business briskly or shrewdly ❶

Watch out, he's a **wheeler-dealer**. He likes to gamble
with money, especially when it's not his own.

**wheels** [wiːlz] *n* any car ❶

You got a set of **wheels** I can borrow?

see also: HOT-ROD, JALOPY

**"when ja"** [wéndʒə] *exp* [from *when did you*] ❶

A: **When ja** go?

B: I went yesterday.

**where one is coming from** [wɛər wʌn iz kʌmiŋ ❸
frʌm] *exp* from one's point of view based on background
or experience

I don't believe in capital punishment, and since you're a
pacifist, I think you know **where I'm coming from**.

**"whew!"** [hiuː] *inter* expression of fatigue, frustration, ❶
surprise, relief

**Whew**! Look at that <u>girl</u> over there with the beautiful
long legs.

**Whew**, I'm <u>beat</u>. I think I'll take a shower and then go
to bed.

**Whew**! You scared me! You shouldn't grab people from
behind like that.

**Whew**! I'm glad that test is over!

see also: PHEW

**white-bread** [wáit bred] *adj* boring, conventional ❸

I don't want some kind of **white-bread** life living in
some house in some suburb. I want to live in New York
City and experience many different cultures.

**white trash** [wait træʃ] *n* an insulting term for poor, ❹
ignorant whites

All the people living in this trailer park are **white
trash**.

see also: REDNECKS

**whiz** [wiz] *n* [from *wizard*] one who possesses a great ❶ skill

My sister is a <u>real</u> **whiz** at math. She started college when she was fourteen.

**whole shebang (the)** [ðə houl ʃəbǽŋ] *n* everything ❶

They had everything at their wedding, a band, a beautiful cake, a sit-down dinner... <u>you know</u>, **the whole shebang**.

**wicked** [wíkəd] *adj* of exceptional quality or degree ❶

This car is **wicked** <u>cool</u>.

see also: TOTALLY

**wild** [waild] *adj* extreme, exciting ❸

That roller coaster was <u>really</u> **wild**. Let's do it again!

see also: AWESOME, BAD, BADASS, CRAZY-ASS, EXCELLENT, INTENSE, OUT OF SIGHT, OUT OF THIS WORLD, RAD, SUPER, TO DIE FOR

**willies (the)** [ðə wíliːz] *n* fear, nervousness, ❶ the jitters

I don't like looking at dead things. It gives me **the willies**.

see also: CREEPS, JITTERS

**willy** [wíliː] *n* penis ❸

He's got a small **willy**.

see also: COCK, DICK, JOHNSON, PECKER, PRICK, WEENIE

**"will ya?"** [wíl jə] *inter* [from *will you*] expression of ❶ urgency or irritation

Hurry up **will ya?** We're very late.

Please stop talking, **will ya?** I can't sleep when there's a <u>racket</u>.

**wimp** [wimp] *n* a weak and timid person ❶

I was surprised to see John so afraid of a snake. I didn't think a two-hundred pound rugby player could be such a **wimp**.

When it comes to horror movies I'm a **wimp**. I can't stand the sight of blood.

I won't marry a **wimp**. I want a <u>real man</u>.

see also: WUSS

**wimp out on** [wimp áut ɔn] *v* to take the easiest ❶
course of action

We had planned to go parasailing yesterday, but Eric **wimped out on** us.

see also: BACK OUT, BAG IT, BLOW OFF, CHICKEN OUT, COLD FEET, COP OUT, DITCH, WALK OUT ON

**wimpy** [wímpi:] *adj* timid, weak ❶

Don't act so **wimpy**. I'll pull the bandage off quickly and you won't feel a thing.

Stop crying <u>will ya?</u> Here's your stupid hat back. <u>God</u>, I can't believe what a **wimpy** <u>cry-baby</u> you are.

see also: CHICKEN, GUTLESS

**wing it** [wíŋ it] *v* to improvise ❶

I didn't have time to prepare my speech, so I had to **wing it**.

We're <u>gonna</u> have to **wing it** tomorrow. We don't have time to practice before the concert.

**wino** [wáinou] *n* someone who is chronically addicted ❶
to drinking wine

A **wino** in the park asked us for money so he could buy some <u>booze</u>.

see also: LUSH

**wiped out** [waipt áut] *adj* exhausted                    ❸

We felt <u>really</u> **wiped out** after cycling all day.

> see also: BEAT, BLEARY-EYED, BURNED OUT, BUSHED, DEAD,
> FRAZZLED, FRIED, OUT OF IT, POOPED, WASTED,
> ZONKED OUT

**wipe out** [waip áut] *v* to have an accident, to fall or    ❸
crash

Matthew **wiped out** when he was skiing and broke his
shoulder.

The driver **wiped out** on the icy road and crashed his
car into a tree.

**wipeout** [wáip aut] *n* a bad fall or accident             ❸

A: Hey <u>dude</u>, did you fall? You're <u>like</u>, <u>totally</u> covered
   with mud.

B: <u>Yeah</u>, it was a <u>total</u> **wipeout** <u>man</u>.

**wired** [waird] *adj* feverishly excited and energized       ❶

He was feeling <u>totally</u> **wired** after drinking three
cappuccinos.

**wise** [waiz] *adj* impertinent, rude, disrespectful         ❶

Don't get **wise** with me young man, or I'll smack you
one across the face.

> see also: FRESH

**wise guy** [wáiz gai] *n* an annoying, self-assured          ❶
person; a practical joker

Who's the **wise guy** who left the beer in the freezer?

> see also: SMART ALECK

**witch** [witʃ] *n* an unpleasant girl or woman               ❶

I can't believe what a **witch** that <u>girl</u> is.

> see also: BITCH

**womanizer** [wúmənaizər] *n* a man who pursues ❶
multiple casual relationships with women.

You think he likes you? Don't be naive Sharon, he's just
a **womanizer**. Once he sleeps with you he'll start
treating you like <u>shit</u> and throw you away like a piece
of garbage.

> see also: DON JUAN, LADY'S MAN

**woody** [wúdi:] *n* erection ❹

He got a **woody** as soon as she took her blouse off.

> see also: BONER, HARD-ON

**workaholic** [wərkəhɔ́lik] *n* a compulsive worker ❶

Tom is a <u>total</u> **workaholic**. He spends his entire
weekends at the office.

**work out** [wərk aut] *v* to solve, develop ❶

He still has some emotional problems that he is trying
to **work out**.

Right now they're just separated, and thinking about
divorce. They're still trying to **work** things **out**.

I hope things **work out** for you in New York.

**works (the)** [ðə wərks] *n* all of the options, ❶
everything

A: What would you like on your hamburger sir?

B: Give me lettuce, tomatoes, <u>ya know</u>, **the works**.

**worst nightmare** [wərst náitmɛər] *n* the most ❶
terrifying possible adversary or outcome

Superman is a criminal's **worst nightmare**.

A fire after a major earthquake is our **worst nightmare**.

**"wow!"** [wau] *inter* expression of amazement or surprise ❶

**Wow**, he's <u>gorgeous</u>! Is he a friend of yours?

**Wow**, I can't believe I ate the whole thing.

**wrap up** [wræp ʌp] *v* to finish ❶

<u>Wow</u>, it's late. Why don't we **wrap** things **up** and go home?

**wreck** [rek] *n* a person whose health or spirits are broken, something that is in a state of ruin ❶

Ever since her husband was killed by a bus, she's been an emotional **wreck**.

My life is a **wreck**. I need to get grounded before I can be in a relationship again.

see also: MESS

**wuss** [wus] *n* timid or weak person ❹

<u>C'mon</u> <u>man</u>, hit me! Are you afraid? <u>Man</u>, you're nothing but a **wuss**!

<u>C'mon</u>, don't be a **wuss**. It's your turn to jump off the bridge.

see also: CHICKEN, JELLYFISH, PUSHOVER, WIMP

# X

**X-rated** [eks réidəd] *adj* pornographic, obscene ❶

I went to the video shop and rented a couple of **X-rated** movies.

He's got an **X-rated** calendar on his desk.

His mind is full of **X-rated** thoughts.

# Y

**ya** [jə] *exp* [from *you*]                                          ❶

How are **ya**?

**yak/yap** [jæk, jæp] *v* talk incessantly, to chatter    ❶

Why do teenagers **yak** on the phone so much?

She **yapped** on the phone for an hour.

>   see also:  BLAB, GAB

**yeah** [jeə] *adv* [from *yes*]                              ❶

A: <u>Ya</u> hungry?

B: **Yeah**, I'm starving. Let's go eat something.

**"yeah, right"** [jeə rait] *inter* sarcastic expression of   ❶
disagreement

A: Yesterday I met two beautiful Swedish models at a
bar and they both fell <u>totally</u> in love with me.

B: **Yeah, right**. You're <u>full of it</u>.

>   see also:  FAT CHANCE, FORGET IT, VERY FUNNY, WHATEVER

**yes-man** [jés mæn] *n* an underling who always agrees  ❶
with a superior

The boss likes to surround himself with **yes-men**.

**"yikes!"** [jaiks] *inter* expression of amazement or   ❶
surprise

**Yikes**! Today's my father's birthday. I almost forgot to
call him.

**"yo!"** [jou] *inter* [from *Hey, you!*] used to call attention ❶
or express affirmation

**Yo!** Get your hands off my car!

**Yo** <u>man</u>, how <u>ya</u> doin?

**"you bet"/"you betcha"** [juː bet, juː bétʃə] *inter* ❶
[from *you bet your ass*] expression of certainty

A: You <u>gonna</u> go camping with us?

B: **You bet**. I love camping.

    see also:  YEAH, YUP

**"you can say that again"** [juː kən sei ðæt əgen] ❶
*inter* "I completely agree with what you said"

A: I think it's time to go home.

B: **You can say that again**. I'm <u>bushed</u>.

**you know/ya know** [juː nou, jə nou] *inter* [from ❶
*as you know*] conversational filler

He's, **ya know**, the <u>best-looking guy</u> in the school.

**Ya know**, I think you're, **ya know**, <u>really</u> pretty.

<u>Dad</u>, I, <u>uh</u>, <u>I mean</u>, <u>uh</u>, **ya know**, I got a date tomorrow.
So can I, <u>uh</u>, <u>like</u>, **ya know**, borrow the car?

    see also:  I MEAN, LIKE

**"you know what I'm saying?"** [juː nou wʌt aim ❶
séijiŋ] *inter* "Don't you agree?" "Do you understand
what I'm telling you?"

I think I need a vacation. **You know what I'm saying?**

**"you name it"** [ju: néim it] *exp* anything one can ❶
think of

What do you want for your birthday? I'll give you
whatever you want. **You name it** and it's yours.

A: What do they sell at Macy's?
B: **You name it**. They've got everything.

**yucky** [jʌ́ki:] *adj* offensive, distasteful ❷
I think tofu is **yucky**.

see also: GNARLY, GRODY, GROSS, ICKY

**yummy** [jʌ́mi:] *adj* pleasing, delectable ❷
That cake looks **yummy**!

**"yup"** [jʌp] *adv* "yes" ❶
A: Are you hungry?
B: **Yup**. Actually, I'm <u>starving</u>.

**yuppie** [jʌ́pi:] *n* [from *young urban professional*] ❶
a well-paid, young, college-educated, white-collar
worker

She likes **yuppies** because they're usually rich.

see also: PREPPIE

# Z

**zero** [zí:rou] *n* something worthless, having no value ❶
Sometimes I feel like such a **zero**. I've done nothing
with my life.

**zilch** [ziltʃ] *n* zero, nothing ❶

A: How much money do you have in your wallet?
B: **Zilch**. I'm <u>flat broke</u>.

see also: DICK, DIDDLY, SQUAT, ZIP

**zillion** [zíljən] *n* a very large number or amount ❶

There are a **zillion** different reasons why I love you.

see also: JILLION, UMPTEEN

**zinger** [zíŋər] *n* a witty remark or retort, anything ❶
causing surprise or shock

That was definitely one of the funniest jokes I ever
heard. It was a <u>real</u> **zinger**.

see also: DOOZY

**zip** [zip] *n* zero, nothing ❶

The score was three to **zip**.

see also: DICK, DIDDLY, SQUAT, ZILCH

**zit** [zit] *n* a pimple ❸

Oh no! I'm getting a **zit** on my nose and the party is
tomorrow! What am I <u>gonna</u> do?

**zombie** [zɑmbiː] *n* a person markedly strange in ❶
appearance or behavior

Don't wander around the house like a **zombie** all day.
Go out and get some exercise.

**zone out** [zoun aut] *v* to daydream, become oblivious ❸
to one's surroundings

He's the most boring teacher I've ever had. Whenever
he talks I just **zone out**.

see also: SPACE OUT

255

**zonked out** [zɑŋkt aut] *adj* tired, exhausted  ❸

When I finish writing a book like this one, I feel **zonked out** for days.

see also:  BEAT, BLEARY-EYED, BURNED OUT, BUSHED, DEAD, FRAZZLED, FRIED, OUT OF IT, POOPED, WASTED, WIPED OUT

**Z's** [ziːz] *n* sleep  ❸

I'm <u>gonna</u> go home now and get some **Z's**

see also:  SHUT-EYE, CATCH SOME Z'S